Contents

Henry Drucker

BREAKAWAY

The Scottish Labour Party

For Paul

EDINBURGH
EUSPB

ISBN 0 904919 19 6 (casebound)
ISBN 0 904919 20 X (paperback)

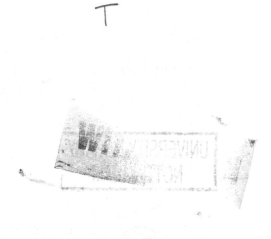

Typeset: 10/12 Times by EUSPB
Printed in Scotland by Lindsay & Co., Edinburgh

Preface

This book is a study of an episode in recent Scottish political history — the creation and first months of the Scottish Labour Party. The party was formed early in 1976 by a revolt of Jim Sillars MP and a group of his friends against the Labour Party. The creation of the party, the need for which had been frequently discussed by Sillars and a group of journalists for some time beforehand, was an immediate sensation. Helped by the flattering and intense publicity it received, it grew to have nearly nine hundred members in forty two branches by the time of its first annual Congress in October 1976. In the process of growing the SLP acquired active support from people who had no previous political affiliation as well as from former SNP members, from two Trotskyist groups, and, most of all, from former members of the Labour Party.

Although its soundest base was in Sillars' home county — Ayrshire, the party attracted support from all over Scotland. If nothing else, it demonstrated in its early days that there was a fair amount of unused political talent in Scotland (as perhaps in the rest of Britain). Then, just as it should have been consolidating its achievement, the SLP exploded, scattering debris over the political landscape. Some members were expelled; more left in anger at the expulsions; still others drifted away when they were convinced that the party was just another 'wee bitty to the left of the Labour Party' organisation.

This study is an attempt to record these dramatic events and to draw lessons from the experience. The SLP was created to combine socialism and nationalism in a new party. Will the gap it sought to fill remain vacant for long? The SLP thrived — for a while — on good press coverage. How long can a publicity campaign succeed? The new party sought to attract voters by emblazoning both 'Socialism' and 'Scotland' on its banner. Can the two be combined? It was deprived of an early General Election which might have tested the notion that there is a large pool of untapped support for another 'Socialist' party. Is there? The party was dominated by its founder. Can new political parties be sustained unless they are highly democratic in their organisation? The SLP's founders set out to use elections as their means of acquiring power, they eschewed community politics and class-struggle politics. Is there not room for a combination of electoral and other campaigns by a new party? The party attracted support from Trotskyist organisations. Is there any way to deal with such supporters short of expelling them?

When I set out to study the SLP I had no intention of writing a book about it. On the contrary, this book grew out of an attempt to write a paper about the creation of the SLP for an academic journal. Some record of this event ought, I thought, to be available for non-Scots and for future historians and political scientists. But the more I studied the party the more interested in it I became and the more interviews I then scheduled. Before too long I had to face the fact that the material was too interesting to be presented only to a professional audience. In any case, it became clear that the story of the SLP's creation and first months had implications which deserved to be discussed widely.

There are two quite different reasons for the expansion into a book: my own proximity to the SLP and the way it nearly destroyed itself. In the first place I was both geographically and politically close to the SLP. I am, as most of their leaders were before they broke away, an active member of the Labour Party; like them I had become a strong devolutionist. They were much closer to the heart of the Labour Party machine than I; but I was close enough to be sympathetic to their impatience with it. When the SLP was formed I went to several of their public meetings and was forced to recognise that they generated an enthusiasm which was not common at Labour Party meetings. This was a disturbing experience.

The second reason why I expanded my projected paper into this short book was very different. The SLP had a fight. It fought within itself and with the International Marxist Group (IMG). Moreover, as I came to realise, IMG also had a fight within itself. As an observer of the SLP this gave me an advantage which students of political

3

organisations rarely enjoy. Both sides of both fights were only too anxious to convince me of the rightness of their actions, and the wickedness of their opponents'. Moreover, many volunteered documentary evidence of their claims in the form of minutes and records of the SLP and IMG. In this way I have come to possess copies of the Minutes of the SLP's National Organising Committee and National Executive Committee, and much other material as well. I have also received a nearly complete set of IMG's papers for the period when it was involved in the SLP. Thus I am able to depict the struggle within and between these organisations from their own official minutes — at least in outline.

On the other hand, it must be admitted at the outset that this access has led to difficulties. When I set out on my research I had agreeable interviews with Jim Sillars and Alex Neil, the SLP's General Secretary. Since I was then only thinking of writing on the origins of their party I spent little time asking them about later events. When word got back to them that I had uncovered material which led me to consider lines of enquiry unflattering to them, co-operation ceased. Thus I have not been able to get their side of some of the crucial events on which this book is based. It must be understood, in fairness to Sillars and Neil, that I have based my account of what happened in their party on official minutes and on interviews with other people. I regret this turn of events for it must inevitably lead to a certain fuzziness and even inaccuracy in details. However, I have checked this account with as many people as I could, though I cannot and do not claim that it is either complete or completely accurate. That would be an impossible goal for a study of this kind. It will be enough if it provides a coherent account of important events, many of which would otherwise be forgotten, and if it provokes a serious public debate about the lessons of the SLP.

It must be appreciated that the events which this book records were not pleasant; some were very unpleasant. Many of the people who took part are not proud of what they have done. Any researcher who was trying to give more than an anodyne account — and what use would that be? — would have faced the problem of co-operation from some quarter. Already the events of the first months of the SLP have been blown up into myths. I have tried, where possible, to examine them. I believe that one advantage of publishing this study now, is that it may serve to puncture some of these myths. Inevitably, too, important sources of information about the party are vanishing. Branch minute books and other records are beginning to disappear into dustbins. More disturbing, some important events, such as the debates on the emergency resolutions at the SLP's first Congress at Stirling and the expulsions of four branches which followed have been excluded from the official record of the Congress. So while it would be dangerous to try to reach definite conclusions about the party, and I do not try to do so, there is much to be said for attempting to place on record as much evidence as possible before it is lost.

At the end of the text I have listed the books, articles and papers which I have consulted in preparing this book. I have also given a list of the people interviewed. Many of the written papers are cyclostyled and will not be easily available to others. I have, therefore, placed all my copies of this material — along with a large additional quantity of SLP and IMG material which I was not able to use — in the Depository of the Unit for the Study of Government in Scotland, at the University of Edinburgh.

The reader will notice one glaring omission from my list of sources consulted: I have looked carefully through many Scottish newspapers, but have not examined tapes of radio and television broadcasts for the relevant periods. This is unfortunate given that so many people now obtain their news from broadcasts and doubly unfortunate here because my comments on the press coverage I have read is not always flattering to the newspapers. The omission is not the result of prejudice in favour of the BBC and STV. On the contrary, it is, as many previous investigators of the subject will testify, quite impossible to do proper research on radio and television broadcasts. Complete copies of all newspapers published in Scotland (and the main English papers) are kept in the National Library of Scotland. They are also kept in the Mitchell Library and many libraries have microfilm records of the *Scotsman* and *Glasgow Herald*. No similar collection of broadcast tapes exists. Indeed when I asked BBC Scotland for texts of the popular "Good Morning Scotland" programme for the period relevant to this study I was told that they had been inadvertently discarded. Thus it is not simply that records of broadcasts are not publicly available. Sometimes they do not exist. This is an unsatisfactory state of affairs.

I am grateful to John Bochel, Jack Brand, Ray Chalmers, Grant Gordon and Vicky Mason for helping me to check various facts; to the staff of the *Scotsman* and the librarian of the *Glasgow Herald* for helping me to locate some missing bits of the puzzle; to Kathy Brown, Helen Ramm and Moira Smith for typing and re-typing the text; to

5

Jack Brand, James Cornford, Carol Craig, Gerry Finn, Litster Gardiner, Sheila Gilmore, Charlie Gordon, David Johnstone, Stephen Maxwell, Neil MacCormick, Jim Mackenchie, Ian Millar, Roger Mullin, John Nairn, Tom Nairn Don Robertson, Jim Tanner and Neil Williamson and most especially to my publishers for their helpful comments on various parts of earlier drafts of this book. Most of all I am deeply grateful to Nancy Drucker for spending countless evenings editing and re-editing the text with me.
I alone remain responsible for the book.

H. M. Drucker
Edinburgh
December, 1977.

6

Chapter I:

The Roots of Rebellion

Britain was once the very model of a two-party political system. From the end of the Second World War until the 1970's British politics was dominated by two great parties each of which was, in effect, a coalition. The Conservative and Labour Parties alternated in power. The British electorate, with few exceptions, kept this alternation intact by refusing to vote for any other party or combination of parties in sufficient numbers to disrupt the *pas de deux*.

By late 1975, when the Scottish Labour Party (SLP) broke away from the (British) Labour Party all that had changed. Britain had become a 'multiparty' state. Both of the major parties were losing votes and, though less dramatically, Parliamentary seats. Nowhere was this more evident than in Scotland. The change in Scottish politics had been sudden. Until the 1966 General Election Scots voters had marched in step, almost in lock-step, with other British voters. But in Parliamentary by-elections after the 1966 General Election, in local government elections and in opinion polls they began to step sharply out of line. The beneficiary was the Scottish National Party (SNP).

The SNP had been formed in 1934. It had spent decades building up a tenacious, widespread organisation of local branches. Alone amongst British parties it came, by the mid-nineteen sixties, to have a thriving local organisation and a weak centre. As the other parties, especially the governing parties, lost local activists so members of the National Party multiplied. When the two governing parties lost credibility in the late 1960's, the National Party was ready to take

7

advantage of the change. During the Parliament elected in 1966 it began to win Parliamentary by-elections and did extremely well in the local government elections of 1967 and 1968. By the time the SLP was formed the SNP had eleven seats in Parliament.

The first victim of the SNP's electoral victories was the Conservative Party. It now seems hard to believe that little more than twenty years ago — in 1955 — the Tories won half the Scottish vote in a General Election. In the October 1974 election it was the third party, reduced to 24.6% of the vote and a mere 16 of the 71 Scottish seats. The SNP came second in votes — taking 30% — and was bidding fair to overtake the Labour Party.

By the end of 1974 everyone in politics could forsee a major constitutional confrontation. If the SNP were to win a majority of Scots parliamentary seats — a feat Labour had accomplished in October 1974 with only 36% of the vote — it would demand negotiations on Scottish independence. Whether it were to win that majority at the next, or the next but one, General Election, hardly mattered. In the new multi-party Scotland the SNP's own strength made an eventual SNP majority seem a near certainty. Thus the rapid shift in electoral allegiances had opened up possibilities of radical constitutional change. How would a Conservative Government elected on an English vote — deal with this challenge? The fact that no one could be sure was an additional factor contributing to the fluidity of Scottish politics.

Hitherto the main bulwark against change has been the Labour Party. The Labour Party in Scotland is based on the apparently unshakeable support of people who live in municipally owned housing, of the trade unions and of the Roman Catholic Church. The proportion of council tenants, trade unionists and Catholics is highest in the cities and towns of West Central Scotland. Labour normally carries them by large majorities. Viewed from a Western European perspective the Labour Party is an anomaly. In no other Western country can the party of the Left count on support from Catholic voters: more important, in no other country of the West are all of the trade unions united behind one Socialist Party. Usually the vote of the organised Left is split among several parties. Not in Scotland.

Could all this be changing? Some people think so. There are signs of decay in the Labour party. Many local constituency parties are controlled by tiny groups of elderly members. Too many local Labour councillors are corrupt, as a series of scandals and court cases has shown. In addition, and despite its ability to win a majority of Scottish Parliamentary seats, the Labour Party is losing votes. Labour's highest vote — 1,283,667 — was cast in 1966. In October 1974 it won 1,000,581. Could it be that, with a Labour Government in office during a period of high unemployment and high inflation, some of the unions would break from the party? In 1975 and 1976 such questions were in the air. Sillars' rebellion from the Labour Party in December 1975 and his creation of the SLP must be seen against this background.

Yet, if there remains one unforgiveable sin in the eyes of most members of the Labour movement, it is betrayal. A movement built on solidarity against powerful enemies knows well the source of its strength. Thus for the man who had the largest Labour majority in Scotland and who was a member of the executive of the Labour Party's Scottish Council to defect required not a little courage. This book is an attempt to explain why and how this happened and to examine the development of the party which he founded.

II

Jim Sillars was born on the 4th of October 1937.[1] His father was a railway man. Jim went to Newton Park School and Ayr Academy. He was a radio operator in the Royal Navy who served mainly in the Far East until he bought himself out and returned to Ayr. There he became a fireman, but was invalided out with knee trouble. He then took up a post with the Fire Brigades Union. Next he served as a full-time Labour Party agent in Ayr, and worked at that job during both the 1964 and 1966 General Elections. He was also a councillor on Ayr Town Council and Ayrshire County Council. Later he served with distinction on the regional hospital board. He became a member of the Transport and General Workers' Union and his last job before being elected an MP was as Head of the Organisation and Social Services Department of the Scottish Trades Union Congress.

Sillars' career is much like that of many other Labour politicians of his generation. His roots go back into the soil of the Labour movement — in his case, into the Ayrshire Socialist movement. He has risen into the bureaucracy of the Labour movement by dint of his considerable wit, charm, ambition, and rhetorical skill. This much is unexceptional. When he broke with the Labour Party he was moving on to new ground. Sillars built the SLP around himself. For this

1. *Who's Who in 1977,* p. 2208.

9

reason alone Sillars and the SLP stood out. In a world of faceless placemen here, it seemed, was a man who had risked his career for a dream.

The dream which inspired Sillars' party is of an independent Socialist Scotland. "We are", he told the inaugural meeting of his party, "Scottish with a capital S and Socialist with a capital S"[2]. The two aspects of the dream were linked. Socialism was thought possible in Scotland only when the English had been shaken off. Moreover, Scotland was thought to be an intrinsically Socialist country so that only Socialists would free it from England. This confidence is entirely explicable in a son of Ayrshire Socialism. For the part of the country he represents has a rock solid Socialist tradition. Labour first won South Ayrshire Constituency in 1918 — it has lost it only once since then — in 1931 when the entire Labour movement was in disarray.

The immediate cause of Sillars' defection from the Labour Party (the 'Old', or the 'British' Labour Party — OLP or BLP as the SLP came to call it) can be found in the Labour government's proposals for devolution. When the break came, it was made by men convinced that the Labour Party was destroying their dream. In November and December 1975 and January 1976 Sillars and his colleagues were on the extreme devolutionist wing of the Labour Party.

Yet this had not always been the case. When he was first elected to Parliament in 1970 Sillars was vehemently opposed to devolution. Sillars' change of mind on this, the main preoccupation of Scottish politics in the 1970's is central to the SLP. Sillars' reasons for establishing the new party can be understood only in relation to the arguments of the time about the devolution of legislative and executive power to an elected Scottish Assembly capable, at least, of running Scotland's 'home' affairs and directing the actions of her civil service. These in turn make sense only in relation to the issue's long history within the Scottish Labour movement.

Labour inherited the long standing Liberal commitment to 'devolution' or 'Home Rule' as it was then usually called, when it inherited so many of the Liberals' Scottish voters in the 1920s. 'Devolution' was repeatedly endorsed by the Labour Party in Scotland. The Labour Party's Scottish Constituency Parties (CLP's) and the Scottish branches of unions affiliated to it have since 1915 held an annual Conference each March to formulate policy and elect an Executive. Resolutions calling for further measures of devolution

2. *Daily Record* 19 January 1976

carried at this Conference on several occasions in the 1920's and the 1940's and in 1951 and 1956.[3]

Then, in 1958, the party in Scotland agreed to a special conference on devolution. This was the time — a rare and painful time— when the Labour Party was re-examining some of its cherished beliefs and rituals. It was a year later that the party leader Hugh Gaitskell tried, unsuccessfully, to get the party to drop its commitment to "nationalise the commanding heights of the economy". The modernisers had more luck in Scotland.

By 1958 it was clear that Labour's oft reiterated commitment to devolution was ritualistic. Little serious had been done about it. Indeed it was becoming an embarrassment. Many Scottish unions had merged with British unions. They saw the whole UK, not Scotland alone, as their field of activity. They recognised that many industries, notably coal and railways, were being subsidised by their respective English parts and came increasingly to believe that the Scottish economy, as a whole, required English subsidies.

The arguments employed against devolution during the special conference which was held in September 1958 were thus largely economic. The arguments in favour of devolution, were mostly the old standbys about 'the Scottish Dimension' and 'a Socialist Scotland'. One argument in favour of devolution, of which much more was to be heard, was that a Scottish Assembly should have county council powers at national level. It was put by a young history lecturer from Edinburgh University: John P. Mackintosh.

On the advice of the Executive the Conference adopted a number of resolutions. The crucial paragraph (No. 4a) read:

We declare our belief in the principle of the maximum possible self-government for Scotland, consistent with the right to remain in the United Kingdom Parliament and continue full representation there. We reject the idea of being separated from the United Kingdom.[4]

It also read that:

The examination of questions affecting (Scottish) Government and Parliament should be undertaken by something in the nature of a Special Committee or Speaker's Conference directly responsible to

3. An excellent account of this history can be found in Keating, Michael J. "Nationalism in the Scottish Labour Movement" (mimeo). See also, Drucker, H. M. 'Devolution and Corporatism" *Government and Opposition,* Summer, pp. 178-193.
4. *Report of the Special Conference of the Scottish Council of the Labour Party,* 13-14 September, 1958. Paragraph 49.

Parliament.[5]

Thus with studied ambiguity the party retreated — "the right to remain in the United Kingdom Parliament and continue full representation there", meant, and was understood to mean, 'no devolution'.

Similar statements were endorsed in 1963, and then again in very different political circumstances in 1968. By 1968 the Scottish National Party (SNP) had established itself as an electoral force. The party won a quite creditable 28.2% of the vote at a by-election in a Glasgow seat (Pollok) in March 1967. Then in November 1967 they won the by-election at Hamilton which established the National Party as a serious electoral force. It also broke through to outstanding victories in local elections in May 1967 and, (though this was yet to come when Labour's Scottish Council met) repeated the performance in May 1968. The devolutionists in the Labour Party saw their chance and pressed it. The Hillhead Constituency Labour party asked the 1968 Scottish conference for a Scottish Parliament. This proposal received derisory support.[6] The matter was remitted to the Executive. In April 1969 Harold Wilson's Government established a Royal Commission on the Constitution under Lord Crowther. After his death, Lord Kilbrandon became chairman.

A streak of perversity affected both Labour and Conservative Parties in their response to the Nationalist threat in the 1960's and early 1970's. In both cases the party leaders in London grasped the electoral danger faster and moved more quickly to head it off than their Scottish followers. The Tory party in Scotland did nothing until the party leader Mr Heath came to the Scottish Conference in Perth in 1968 and told them they were in favour of devolution. To an extent Scottish Labour also waited on London. It was just this kind of perversity in the Labour Party, for which Sillars must take some of the blame, which was eventually to drive him out of it.

In 1969 the Labour Party in Scotland was holding back. In the early part of the year Wilson and his Cabinet had decided that the way to deal with the problem was to set up a Royal Commission. An announcement about the Commission was made on April 1st. Yet only the previous month the Executive of the Scottish Council of the Labour Party was raising strong objections to devolution. Its Chairman, John Pollock, addressed the Conference on devolution

5. *Op.cit.* paragraph 51.
6. *Scotsman,* May 1968, p. 1 and 7.

and used a number of arguments which have been employed repeatedly since. He rejected separation and 'the kind of status accorded to Northern Ireland'. There was, at the time, no Minister for Northern Ireland. The delegates were asked by Pollock to wait for the constitutional commission which would begin with "a re-examination of the whole structure of the UK Parliament". Most important of all, Pollock argued, devolution must be fitted into the new pattern of local government which the Royal Commission on Local Government in Scotland, under the chairmanship of Lord Wheatley, was about to propose.[7] Scottish Labour was sufficiently uneasy about devolution to welcome any excuse for delay.

III

So was Jim Sillars. In March 1968 he was the full-time Agent of the Labour Party in Ayr, a pleasant coastal town south of Glasgow. In that role he had helped Alex Eadie fight the Ayr seat — unsuccessfully — in the 1964 General Election. Eadie subsequently won Midlothian for Labour. Together in 1968 Eadie and Sillars wrote and privately published a 15-page pamphlet 'Don't Butcher Scotland's Future'.[8] The pamphlet began by stressing the need to meet the challenge of the SNP. This, the authors asserted, could best be done by "responding constructively to the obvious wish of Scots to have more to say in Scottish affairs".[9] Yet the tone of the first section was negative. It was about the dangers of separation.

The National Party was castigated for its failure to work out how separation of the closely integrated economies of Scotland and England could be achieved. Without such plans, any separation would amount to a revolution and "a revolution, even when peacefully carried out, is bad for business".[10] Capital would flow out of Scotland. English nationalism would assert itself. English industrialists would be only too pleased to be relieved of government pressure to invest north of the Border. Indeed if Scotland were to separate, England would be more likely to join the Common Market and industry would migrate from Scotland towards the major European markets.

7. Speech by John Pollock in Scottish Government Debate.
8. Eadie, Alex and Sillars, Jim *"Don't Butcher Scotland's Future: the case for reform at all levels of government"* (published privately, 1968).
9. *Op.cit.* p. 3.
10. *Op.cit.* p. 4.

13

And Sillars and Eadie had a stronger argument still. Offshore English gas was about to transform the UK economy as it had transformed the Dutch. Separation it was claimed would "fly in the face of events". If 52 million Britons constituted too small a home market for the new technologically sophisticated industries it was "manifestly crazy for a nation of 5 million to think of contracting out".[11]

In place of separation, Sillars and Eadie placed their hopes on the "regionalisation" of Britain. Any such regional pattern would "have to provide (Scotland and Wales) with additional powers to secure self-determination in broad cultural matters". But they went on to argue against a Scottish Parliament even on a federal basis. Industrial control could be effectively exercised only by a strong central government. Hence the only solution lay in strengthening institutions which could operate in the existing framework. They wanted an additional Select Committee on Scottish Affairs for the House of Commons and a strong two-tier system of local government (much like that which Wheatley recommended and which now operates).

The general lines of the argument of "Don't Butcher Scotland's Future" accorded well with the anti-devolution stance of the Labour Party in the period up to the October 1974 election. Indeed, "Don't Butcher Scotland's Future" is a classic statement of the anti-nationalist and anti-devolutionist case. Labour in Scotland was deeply opposed to nationalism and devolution and Sillars' pamphlet was to place him alongside his fellow Ayrshire MP The Rt. Hon. William Ross, then Secretary of State for Scotland, in the van. The pamphlet, along with Sillars' energetic work as agent in Ayr earned him the descriptive tag which, again, he shared with Ross as 'Hammer of the Nats.' Sillars was soon to get a chance to confirm that reputation.

IV

In addition to being Agent for the Ayr Constituency Labour Party Sillars was also (unpaid) Secretary of the Ayrshire Labour Federation. The federation's purpose was to formulate Labour's policy for the Ayrshire County Council. But it was much more than that. The Ayrshire Labour Federation was a legend in the Labour

11. *Op.cit.* p. 11.

B

Party. It was cited, particularly in Labour strongholds outside the four Scottish cities, as a model to be emulated. It encompassed five parliamentary seats: Ayr Burghs, Bute and North Ayrshire, Central Ayrshire, Kilmarnock and South Ayrshire. In addition to its formal role of making policy for the Labour Party in the county, the Federation approved (or rejected) local government nominations. More important, perhaps, the Federation held regular discussion meetings on most contentious issues within the party. These meetings were attended punctiliously by many Socialists in the county and provided a platform at which ordinary members could argue with councillors and MPs (sometimes Ministers) as equals.

Sillars, as Secretary, was junior to his old friend John Pollock who had long been Chairman. On 18th October 1969 the MP for South Ayrshire that much loved rebel, Emrys Hughes, died. Hughes had represented the seat since 1946. The son-in-law and biographer of Keir Hardie, Hughes was on the extreme nationalist wing of the Labour Party. When in 1967 Mrs Winifred Ewing entered the House of Commons after her by-election victory at Hamilton on behalf of the SNP she had no one from her own party to sponsor her. Hughes and the Welsh nationalist MP Gwynfor Evans came forward as sponsors. Hughes' death created a vacancy which many assumed Pollock would fill. Pollock's long tenure as Chairman of the Federation had created an impression of Parliamentary ambitions which his frequent denials had done nothing to dispel.

So Pollock's refusal to stand in a seat which was safe for Labour took everyone by surprise. In the event there were two candidates: Sillars, who sought and obtained the support of the Young Socialist branches and other local parties, and William Goudie, a much respected local councillor in his forties. Goudie won the NUM nomination. He also had the tacit backing of South Ayrshire's agent Jim Tanner. The NUM's backing alone was expected to be sufficient to win Goudie the nomination. Sillars, then 32 years old, beat Goudie by one vote.

The SNP candidate at the election was Sam Purdie. The by-election was embittered by the fact that Purdie was a renegade. He had been Emrys Hughes' agent at the previous election. Sillars' campaign, at times, developed the themes of "Don't Butcher. . .". He told the Press on March 3rd:

> In my view, nationalism cannot be regarded as a purely orthodox political party movement. History shows that when any country

15

divests itself of empire and falls back on the basic home unit, there is a tendency in the initial phase for tensions to arise in the whole community. I think we are going through this transitional phase at the moment. If allowed to develop too far, it could lead to the dismemberment of the whole United Kingdom. Economic dismemberment would be disastrous for Scotland and — socially and politically — a tragedy for the whole United Kingdom.[12]

But at other times Sillars dwelt on Purdie's betrayal. He made much in a public debate of Purdie's change of heart: was Purdie still a Socialist?[13] One SNP activist told me that he could remember Sillars saying "The Labour movement will never support a turncoat". Several journalists remember it as a particularly bitter campaign: a number of them spent much of the campaign in South Ayrshire. Despite the bitterness of the fight it was during this campaign when so much attention was focussed on the normally quiet seat in the coal-mining county south west of Glasgow, that some of Sillars friendships with Scotland's political journalists began. Stewart MacLachlan now Political Reporter of the *Daily Record* and a founding member of the SLP and others were first drawn to Sillars during this by-election.

The poll was held on the 19th of March. The result pleased Labour. In this seat which has a tradition of high polls 75% of the 50,866 electors turned out. More than half of those who voted, — 20,664 — voted Labour. The Conservative candidate won 9,778 votes, two thousand less than in the previous election. Purdie, the Nationalists' first candidate in the seat polled 7,785 (20%) and came third. Sillars' victory was hailed as a defeat for the SNP and for devolution. An enthusiastic Secretary of State, hailed Sillars' achievement. In the *Daily Record* he was quoted as saying "I'm sure in twenty years Jim Sillars will be sitting in my (Cabinet) seat".[14]

Five years later Neal Ascherson Scottish Political Correspondent of the *Scotsman* was to pick up that thought and use it in a profile of Sillars: "Jim Sillars: a future Prime Minister of Scotland?"[15] It is characteristic of Sillars that people have recourse to extremes when describing him. He invokes strong feelings. Some of his friends have even used religious metaphors. Ascherson, for instance, in his

12. **Cumnock Chronicle**, 6 March, 1970.
13. **Cumnock Chronicle**, 27 February, 1970.
14. **Daily Record**, 18 March, 1970.
15. Ascherson, N. "Jim Sillars: a future Prime minister of Scotland?", **Scotsman**, 1 November, 1975, p. 6.

'profile' referred to Sillars' conversion (on devolution) as "from Saul to Paul". Bob Brown, first Chairman of the SLP told me about Sillars' speech at the Inaugural Meeting of the SLP in biblical terms, "Jim Sillars was John the Baptist".[16]

Perhaps one reason for the strong feelings Sillars invokes is the strong language he uses himself. Two days after the *Scotsman* ran a leader which disapproved of "Don't Butcher Scotland's Future" it printed a letter from him which said:

> We agree with you that our arguments will cut little ice with many Nationalists. Many are, unfortunately like your leader writer, beyond intellectual redemption. . .[17]

This letter illustrates another feature of Sillars' character upon which his friends often remark: he doesn't take criticism well. He has an old-fashioned rigid, very Scottish, schoolmasterly pride, and yet this charming and mercurial man can on occasion change his mind very quickly. More than once in the early days of the SLP, most especially at its first Congress in Stirling in October 1976, Sillars' character made a deep mark on his party.

It wasn't long after his election in 1970 that Sillars was expressing his disillusionment with Parliament and Westminster. By the June 1970 General Election he was already worried. There were two factors. Firstly, "Westminster didn't take Scotland seriously" — "They took the Scottish Labour voter for an idiot" — "They were treating us like a political peasantry".[18] In addition he was annoyed by the way the 1970 General Election was fought: Labour, he said, made promises to voters in Scotland which it didn't mention in England. Nevertheless he was returned by the electors of South Ayrshire with a handsomely increased vote.

Sillars' doubts about the Labour Party increased in subsequent months. His doubts about the wisdom of its devolution policy and the line he had taken in "Don't Butcher Scotland's Future" were quickened by the result of the next by-election in a Scottish Parliamentary seat: Falkirk and Stirling Burghs — in September 1971.

Falkirk and Stirling was, like South Ayrshire, considered a safe Labour seat. But Falkirk and Stirling was near to the area in Central Scotland between Glasgow and Edinburgh where the SNP had been working hard for years. At the 1966 General Election the Labour candidate won 53% of the votes, the Conservative candidate came

16. Interview with Bob Brown March 1977.
17. **Scotsman** 15 March, 1968. The **Scotsman** commented on the letter that it was "as naive and specious as his pamphlet".
18. Interview with Jim Sillars April, 1977. These were remarks he often repeated to others.

second with 31% and the Nationalists were a poor, but not negligible, third with 15%. This indeed was one of their best performances. In 1970 Labour won 51% of the votes while again the Conservative candidate came second with 35%. The Nationalist performance, after all the excitement in the intervening period, was virtually identical to the 1966 performance — 14%. It is little wonder then that Labour's candidate Harry Ewing, a long associate of Alex Eadie's, was startled when the Nationalists came second in the by-election with 35% of the vote.

Could this result have shaken the confidence of the Labour group? Certainly when Ewing went to Westminster it was with a conviction that something had to be done to stop the Nationalists. Ewing joined Eadie and Sillars and the three became very close. It was at this point that the arguments in favour of devolution began to reinforce one another. The Nationalist challenge had to be answered and the fact of European entry changed the argument. Now Scotland could be legally independent of England and yet tied to her economically and politically by virtue of membership of the Common Market. Thus at a blow the Nationalists could be outmanoeuvred; Scotland could have her legal independence with all the attendant psychological and cultural advantages while suffering few if any economic disadvantages. This argument came to be very important in the Scottish Labour Party.

Chapter II:

A Mini Cadre of Hard Line Devolutionists

Meanwhile the devolution argument continued to develop. In the first place, the General Election of 1970 returned a Conservative Government while Scotland elected a majority of Labour MPs. The Nationalist poll was much lower than their local government victories of 1968 and 1969 had suggested it would be and only one Nationalist MP, Donald Stewart in the Western Isles, was returned. The Royal Commission on the Constitution continued its deliberations until 1973 and the Conservatives' Constitutional Committee under Sir Alec Douglas Home reported in 1972. Both recommended a degree of devolution, the Royal Commission under Lord Kilbrandon eventually advocated a directly elected single chamber Assembly sitting in Edinburgh and having both legislative and executive powers.

For the devolutionists, Kilbrandon was a big step forward. The backing of a Royal Commission was useful when the voters temporarily turned away from the National Party. An even bigger step forward was taken when the SNP won a by-election at Govan in November 1973. However, largely because Labour's London headquarters thought the Nationalist threat was dead, Labour fought the February 1974 General Election with no manifesto commitment to devolution. At that election the Nationalist vote revived and Labour fought the October 1974 election with an explicit promise to create an elected Assembly. The first detailed picture of what that Assembly would look like was contained in the Government's White Paper of November 1975. It was the publication of this White Paper which sparked off Sillars' rebellion from the Labour Party.

19

Some rebellions are spontaneous. They erupt in a moment of outrage and frustration. In this sense the rebellion which led to the formation of the SLP was spontaneous. It broke out immediately after the publication of the White Paper on devolution, 'Our Changing Democracy' (*Cmnd.* 6348) and was in part an impatient protest against the betrayal of hopes which that document revealed. Certainly the vast majority of the hundreds of mostly young people who joined the party in the exciting months after its inauguration in January 1976 acted without calculated forethought.

But that is only part, and, as it turned out, the least important part of the truth. The idea which became the SLP and the determination to form it had been conceived, argued about, evolved, and finally launched at a series of meetings which were held between the Stirling and Falkirk by-election in September 1971 and the public announcement of the SLP in December 1975. The meetings became regular. They were attended by four MPs — Eadie, Ewing, Robertson (MP for Paisley) and Sillars — and a number of journalists. In time the character of the group changed, but throughout Sillars was the dominant MP and Bob Brown was the dominant journalist. Brown had been the *Times'* first Scottish correspondent. He later moved to the *Guardian*, contributed regularly to the *Economist* and was News Editor of the *Glasgow Herald* before becoming the Information Officer of the University of Strathclyde. At the time of these secret meetings Brown and Hamish McKinven also served as (unpaid) Press Officers of the Labour Party's Scottish Council's Executive. Brown became, for a short time, the SLP's first Chairman. He often deputised, after retiring from the Chair, for the new Chairman, Don Robertson, when Robertson could not attend meetings. After October 1976 Brown became one of the SLP's two Press Officers.

Another important member of the group which conceived and launched the SLP was Alex Neil. Neil was to become the General Secretary of the SLP at its foundation. Neil was an Honours graduate of the University of Dundee — in whose student politics he first came to prominence. On behalf of the University's Labour Club he had organised a rent-strike when the University attempted to impose a large rise in rents for student accommodation. In this role Neil demonstrated considerable organisational flair and boundless energy; he also fell out with the other, more Left-wing, student leaders when the strike did not succeed. Neil became the Labour Party's Scottish Council's Research Officer in May 1974. He was in a

20

key position from then until his resignation in December 1975 to see how the argument in the Labour Party was developing.

James Frame of the (Edinburgh) *Evening News* and an old friend of Bob Brown's was close to the heart of the group from the beginning. He was later to become a member of the SLP's National Organising Committee and subsequently to be a Press Officer of the party. Other journalists who were to become prominent in the party, such as Jim Fyfe of the *Glasgow Herald*, were recruited to the group at a late stage. Fyfe was also to be, for a short time, a member of the SLP's National Organising Committee. Chris Baur a journalist first with the *Scotsman*, at the time of these meetings with the *Financial Times*, and subsequently the Scottish Political Correspondent of the BBC, was much respected by the members of this group and often consulted by them. He never joined the SLP.[1]

In June 1975 Neal Ascherson, Scottish Political Correspondent of the *Scotsman* (who was not involved in the private meetings) dated them back to 1971, 'after four years of preparation . . .'.[2] Bob Brown confirmed the date. Alex Neil pointed out that the meetings were irregular at first, perhaps every month or, sometimes, every third month. Jim Fyfe remembers them as more frequent, perhaps every six weeks.[3]

After the February 1974 election, Eadie and Ewing ceased to meet with the group. Eadie had become a Minister and Ewing was to become one after the October election. From this time on, the focus of the meetings became clearer. Before the 1974 elections the group were mainly concerned to reform the Labour Party in Scotland — though the need to establish a separate Scottish Labour Party if it did not change was discussed. After the 1974 elections the group came increasingly to believe that the Labour Party was bound to destroy itself — perhaps over the European question, if not that, then certainly over the Scottish question — and that a new Scottish Socialist party would have to be formed. Increasingly too, they came to believe that they should form it. As a result Sillars became even more dominant within the group. For the journalists realised that if an independent Scottish Labour Party was ever to be created, it would be Sillars — the politician — not they — the journalists who would take the risks — so they had to defer to his opinion.[4]

1. This paragraph is based on interviews with Baur, Brown, Frame, Fyfe and Neil.
2. Ascherson, N. "Sillars Goes It Alone", *Scotsman*, 10 June 1975.
3. Interview with Jim Fyfe, June 1977.
4. Interview with Bob Brown, March 1977.

At the same time, Bob Brown's role as a paternal moving force is not to be overlooked. In his late forties at the time, Brown was older than the other central figures and was much respected by all in the group. A direct, emphatic, unyielding man, Brown also had the great moral advantage of consistency: he had always believed the Labour Party in Scotland needed more autonomy. He had never really accepted the decision of 1958: he was a long standing devolutionist. Brown traces his fervent belief in the 'Scottish Dimension', as he puts it, to an earlier tradition of Scottish Socialism. Sillars was later to say that the "SLP was historically and politically inevitable". The notion that an SLP was historically and politically inevitable was pure Bob Brown; the decision to create this SLP in December 1975 was Jim Sillars'.

So at first the group — this "mini-cadre" as Brown was to characterise it — was little more than a group of like-minded Labour Party politicians and journalists who met to discuss plans and concert action on devolution. In time they became a 'maximalist' pressure group (i.e. they always wanted more devolution, no matter how much was on offer). The notion of a breakaway party gained ground in their ranks only after the second 1974 General Election. Only then did the group become anything like a conspiracy.

Yet even when the group decided upon a break from the Labour Party, planning for their own new party remained sketchy. They never resolved the question of whether their party was to be a permanent competitor to the Labour Party or just a temporary expedient around which the remnants in Scotland of a defeated Labour Party — annihilated at the polls by the SNP — would reform. They gave too little thought to raising money for the party and devoted no effort to securing Sillars' base in South Ayrshire. For a long time after his break, Sillars clung to the hope that if he did not 'do a Taverne' (Dick Taverne, MP for Lincoln had resigned from the Labour Party to form his own party and resigned his seat to force a by-election — which he won against an official Labour Party candidate) Labour might not excommunicate him.[5]

A little more thought on the part of the Sillars group would have revealed such hopes to be in vain. But the hope of a successful break was kept alive in the context of this enclosed group.

---

5. A good many of the commonplace phrases of the mini-cadre were reported in the *Scotsman* in its reports of 10 December 1975 to 18 January 1976.

The first fruit of the mini-cadre's meetings was a twenty-one page discussion paper, 'Scottish Labour and Devolution'. Bearing the names of Eadie, Ewing, Robertson and Sillars, the pamphlet was published privately in 1974.[6]

The new paper reversed the arguments of 'Don't Butcher Scotland's Future'. As recent converts to the devolutionist cause, Sillars and Eadie were impatient with their previous faith and with its adherents.

In its introduction, the pamphlet urged that Labour 'should firmly establish itself now as a party with a clearly defined policy' (for devolution). Early on the pamphlet takes a coy nod backwards at 'Don't Butcher . . .'. The authors had come to regard the case for devolution as a sound one . . . 'after years of study, thought, self-debate and a fundamental reappraisal of previously held views'. The crucial point was then underlined:

> The pamphlet deliberately argues the case for devolution of substantial powers from the Westminster Parliament to an elected Assembly in Edinburgh. The ideas are in support of devolution, not separation. The underlying wish is to see the United Kingdom continue as one State, and the British Labour movement continue as one movement.[7]

This was the first published hint that Sillars' group was considering the constitution of the Labour movement as well as that of the United Kingdom.

In the first part of the pamphlet the authors tried to awaken the Labour Party to the electoral consequences of devolution. As they saw it, the Stirling and Falkirk (1971) and Govan (1973) by-elections showed that the electorate wanted the Labour Party to favour devolution and would punish the party if it did not. The authors also speculated that the nationalist feelings which had provoked these by-election warnings had been strengthened by 'a forced entry into the EEC'. As politicians appealing to other politicians the authors had the sense to know that an appeal to electoral self-preservation would count for more than arguments about good government. This alone

6. Eadie, Alex; Ewing, Harry; Robertson, John and Sillars, Jim, *Scottish Labour and Devolution: A discussion paper 1974.*
7. Eadie, Alex *et al, Op. cit.* p. 1.

could justify their decision to put this argument in the first section. And yet the arrangement of the pamphlet strengthens the suspicion that their conversion was not the principled decision they claimed: they too wanted to be on the winning side.

In the second and third parts of the pamphlet the authors declared themselves to be in sympathy with the general outlines of the Kilbrandon proposals save that they wanted more economic power for the Assembly than Kilbrandon had proposed. They also wanted Britain to renegotiate the terms on which she entered the EEC. but not at the expense of directing attention away from the Scottish issue.

They reckoned that the Conservative Party was unlikely ever to control the Assembly; certainly it was less likely to control the Assembly than Westminster. They also believed that the then Conservative administration was maladministering Scotland. Thus subjects devolved would also be subjects protected against Conservative rule. As they put it:

> It would be an extremely foolish person indeed who would count on never having a Tory (Westminster) administration governing in Scotland again.[8]

On the other hand, an Assembly:

> . . . would provide a new focus of political interest and power, and give a new purpose to living in and working for Scotland.[9]

In view of "Don't Butcher's" proposal for an additional Select Committee of the House of Commons to handle Scottish affairs, it was a bit unkind of "Scottish Labour and Devolution" to berate the Scottish Council of the Labour Party so heavily for proposing much the same thing.

In its final short sections, "Scottish Labour and Devolution", (1) restated its opposition to separatism, (2) elaborated its view on the need for an economic role for a Scottish Assembly, (3) proposed a revenue-based development fund, (4) denied that an Assembly was 'a slippery slope' to separation and (5) affirmed that Scotland 'is one of the areas of Britain in which the idea of socialism has a firm grip'. In

8. *Op. cit.* p. 12.
9. *Ibid.*

short, it propounded the main lines of what were to become SLP policies.

III

The members of the informal devolutionist group, politicians and journalists alike, fought the two 1974 General Elections from within the Labour Party. Inside the party they were well placed to use its machine to increase the internal pressure for devolution.

In February 1974 the electorate returned a Labour minority administration on a minority of votes. Scottish and English voters alike moved away from the old governing parties. In England, the Liberals were the beneficiaries; in Scotland the National Party gained. Still, Labour retained a majority of Scottish seats. Labour held 40 seats, the Conservatives were reduced to 21, having lost four to the Nationalists, the SNP won 7 seats and the Liberals 3.

The effect of the February election was radically to increase the leverage of the devolutionists. Their argument that Nationalist voters could be contained only by devolution was accepted on all sides. The narrow difference between the large parties in Parliament made both sensitive to the needs of their Scottish constituencies. Labour was particularly vulnerable to this pressure as — with 40 MPs — it had most to lose from further SNP advances. Its hopes of forming a majority administration at the next election, which everyone knew would soon follow, could so easily be lost in Scotland. The Nationalists' seven seats were a poor return for their 23% of the vote — and they held the initiative. Sillars was offered a place in Harold Wilson's Government — he could have had a junior Ministerial post in the Department of Health and Social Security. A more senior post in the Scottish Office might have tempted him. Sillars turned down the Prime Minister's offer.

Labour's February 1974 Manifesto had been silent on the subject of devolution. Between the elections of 1974 the party adjusted itself and agreed to a commitment on the subject. Parliament had hardly assembled when the Executive (EC) of the Scottish Council of the Labour Party took the first grudging steps. It issued a statement which said:

> We welcome Kilbrandon's emphatic rejection of the Nationalist case.
> We do, however, accept that there is a real need to ensure that
> decisions affecting Scotland are taken in Scotland wherever

25

possible.[10]

That this statement hardly betokened a wholehearted commitment to devolution goes without saying. The difficulty was that the EC contained a good many members who were still strongly opposed to the concept of an elected Assembly. Nevertheless, they were out-voted on this occasion. The next day the Prime Minister could appoint his old friend, Lord Crowther-Hunt, to advise Ministers on devolution. Given that Crowther-Hunt was a co-author of the Memorandum of Dissent to Kilbrandon, and that the Minority Report had recommended an appreciably greater degree of devolution than the main report, Downing Street's announcement was nicely couched: Crowther-Hunt was to give advice "in connection with work the Government are putting in hand on the recommendations of the majority and minority reports of the Commission on the Constitution".[11]

This was an exasperating period for the devolutionists. In principle, they were opposed to London making decisions which affected Scotland. In practice, they were obliged to count on London to force Scotland to ask for more freedom from London. In turn, this Scottish recalcitrance can only have been infuriating to Labour's Scottish Ministers. For it was at this time that they were fighting the endless battles against the reluctant Treasury for a White Paper — and later a Bill — which would grant a devolution of power. Nothing could have undermined their case more than a divided, taciturn, reluctant Scottish party. Lack of enthusiasm was not, however, a complaint which could be made against the 'maximalists'.

Later in March (the 23rd) the Annual Conference of the Scottish Council went no further than to approve the Executive Committee's grudging statement. But behind this approval there was much manoeuvring and misunderstanding. The conference was faced, in addition to its EC's statement with a resolution hostile to devolution (proposed by the General and Municipal Workers Union (GMWU) and seconded by Paisley Constituency Party), and a number of resolutions in favour of devolution which went beyond the EC's position. The GMWU were agreeable to withdrawing their resolution, but the seconders, Paisley, were not. Conference heavily defeated their resolution. On the other hand, the resolutions strongly backing devolution did not get the support from the large unions

10. *Scotsman*, 12 March 1974, p. 1.
11. *Scotsman*, 13 March 1974, p. 1.

26

which they might have because the mover of the Executive's resolution, Donald Dewar, and the final speaker, John Pollock, convinced them that the Executive was moving in a pro-devolution direction. It seems very likely that if those in favour of devolution in the large unions had realised just how precariously the arguments were balanced in the EC, they would have taken a stronger line. The conference decision was hardly good enough for the pro-devolutionists in general. They applied further pressure from London for a more definite and precise commitment. Early in June the Government issued a discussion document on devolution. Its purpose was to initiate discussion in Scotland, Wales and England on devolution. It offered a variety of schemes and asked for comments. Its most devolutionary scheme — 'A' — was a schematic version of the Kilbrandon Report.

At this point the EC of the Scottish Council threw a wrench into the devolution machine in a way which raised questions about its right to be taken seriously. At a few days' notice, an extraordinary meeting was called for June 22nd. With a bare third of its members present (a World Cup football match involving Scotland was being televised that afternoon), it rejected all of the proposed schemes of devolution which the government had offered by six votes to five. On the following Monday, the *Daily Record* published the vote. Tom Fulton, Donald Dewar, Hugh Brown, George Robertson and Frank Gormill had voted for devolution; Sadie Hatton, David Davidson, Jean McVey, Geoff Shaw, Alan Campbell McLean and Peter Talbot were the majority opponents of any of the government's proffered schemes. Bob Brown told me that the Sillars group was so infuriated by this decision that they nearly broke with the Labour Party there and then.[12]

Their fury was shared by Labour's leaders in London. The Party's National Executive (NEC) and its administrative centre (Transport House) lost all patience with their Scottish colleagues and called the Scottish organiser, Peter Allison, down to London. He was told to see to it that the Scottish Council held a special conference on devolution to reverse the '6-5' vote.

The Executive of the Scottish Council met again on July 8th. It would have been difficult, of course, for Allison to say 'Well, lads, Transport House won't have it — we'll have to call a special conference to get this '6-5' decision changed'. Nerves were too raw for that. Many of those on the Executive who were in favour of

12. Interview with Bob Brown, July 1977.

27

devolution were recent and reluctant converts. So it was very fortunate for Allison, and the devolutionists on the EC, that a number of constituency parties and unions (including the AUEW) had written to the EC demanding a special conference. They backed these demands. The EC was also under pressure from the Press to demonstrate its commitment to devolution. It was enough. A majority agreed that a special conference be called. Allison never mentioned his instructions from Transport House at the meeting.

In the meantime, however, a 'secret' NEC-sponsored opinion poll raised the stakes by showing that Labour would lose thirteen seats in Scotland were it not to change its devolution policy. On the 25th of July, the Party's NEC met in London — with barely a dozen present — and agreed to a motion of Alex Kitson which declared its support for devolution publicly. This decision, taken at the end of the NEC meeting, risked an embarrassing split with the Scottish Council. It also put heavy pressure on the Scottish Council to reverse its EC's decision.

The Special Conference was held on September 16th in the Co-operative Halls, Dalintober Street, Glasgow. 'Dalintober' was Labour at its least happy. The devolutionists got their way by arm twisting. The decision of the NEC in July, the fear of losing seats to the Nationalists, the commitment of the unions not to do anything which would upset the Labour Government's chance of re-election, all had a powerful effect. Many voted cheerlessly for a form of devolution which, in their hearts, they abhorred. The trade unions' block votes were delivered in the main without enthusiasm. All this was galling to Sillars' group and engraved the memory of 'Dalintober Street' on their hearts. More than anything else it determined them not to have trade union block votes in the SLP.

The delegates at the conference were faced with five propositions on which to vote. Propositions 1 and 2 were there to warm them up. Proposition 1 declared opposition to separation. It carried unanimously. Equally unsurprisingly, the second proposition calling for the return of a Labour Government also carried unanimously. The real business of the day was contained in Propositions 3, 4 and 5. Number 3 declared opposition to 'the setting up of a Scottish Assembly as being irrelevant to the needs and aspirations of the people of Scotland'. Someone had done his homework this time. It was defeated overwhelmingly. The 4th proposition was the main subject:

That this conference recognising the desire of the Scottish people for a greater say in the running of their own affairs calls for the setting up of a directly elected Assembly with legislative powers within the context of the political and economic unity of the U.K.[13]

It was carried overwhelmingly. The mountain was moving to Mohammed. Even then the conference passed Proposition 5, which called for the retention of all existing advantages: the 71 MPs and the Secretary of State in the Cabinet. It also declared its opposition to proportional representation. Thus was the way cleared for the Government to issue in September 1974 its first White Paper on devolution called 'Democracy and Devolution; Proposals for Scotland and Wales', which endorsed the main features of the Kilbrandon majority report.

Labour's Manifesto for the October election promised that "the next Labour Government will create elected assemblies in Scotland and Wales" For the first time the party also produced a Manifesto for Scotland.[14] It acknowledged the demands of Scottish people for a greater voice in running their own affairs and said that substantial powers over the crucial areas of decision-making in Scotland would be devolved. At the same time the party stated its belief that the Scottish people did not want the separation advocated by the SNP. An Assembly of real status and power with directly elected Assemblymen was contrasted with the Conservative proposals. Naturally, there was to be no reduction in the number of Scottish MPs at Westminster and proportional representation was ruled out. When it came to describe just what areas the Assembly would control the Manifesto was less clear. Certainly it would be concerned with all the areas then administered by the Scottish Office. But on what was then becoming the battleline between the 'minimalists' and the 'maximalists' — economic policy — the Manifesto marched both ways at once. The recently created Scottish Development Agency was responsible to the Secretary of State. Would the Assembly control it? The Scottish Manifesto noted:

> In the trade and industry field, Labour has already moved more decision-making to Scotland. The Scottish Development Agency will be a vital addition to Scottish power in this field. The Agency will, of course, be in operation before an Assembly is established. It will be responsible to the Secretary of State for Scotland, and when the

13. Report of the Special conference of the Scottish Council of the Labour Party 1975. Proposition No. 4.
14. Although it produced separate documents (which were not called 'manifestos') for Scotland in the 1950, 1959 and 1964 General Elections. See F. W. S. Craig. British General Election Manifestos 1900-1974. (London. 1975). p. 484 — who. however, lists these earlier documents as 'manifestos'.

29

Assembly is later set up, it may become appropriate to make the Agency responsible to the Assembly.[15]

In any case, even if control of the SDA were given to the Assembly, the Manifesto went on to observe:

> Of course, there will be many areas — for example, defence, foreign affairs, and major questions of economic policy — where the U.K. Government will remain responsible.[16]

This Scottish Manifesto was an amalgam of the national Manifesto and some local material. The local material was the responsibility of Bruce Millan MP (then a senior Minister in the Scottish Office) and Alex Neil. Both had a hand in it but it was colloquially known as 'Alex's' — and to that extent it was the product of the thinking of the 'mini-cadre'. There were complaints, nonetheless, that the Scottish Manifesto had been written in London and shown to the Scottish Executive only when it was too late to make any major changes. However this may be, the 'mini-cadre' had a further role in the election campaign.

The Labour Party reserves a special place in its theology for manifestos which are held in awe and reverence. A promise made in a manifesto is held to be literally binding on the Government elected. One of the weaknesses of this theory is that very few people read, let alone remember, what is in manifestos. Thus they become a kind of esoteric text which must be vulgarised for the politically unsophisticated electorate. In Scotland the people who performed this vulgarisation were, many of them, members of Sillars' private group.

The two main texts of Labour's 1974 October campaign were a news-sheet 'Labour News' and a televised party political broadcast which was shown on 7th October (polling took place on the 10th). Both were written or influenced by maximalists on the devolution issue. 'Labour News', a four-page broadsheet which the party proposed to deliver to each Scottish household, was written by the 'mini-cadre'. It employed the simple format and literary style, which in Scotland is normally associated with the *Daily Record* (also Labour — it is Scotland's version of the *Daily Mirror*) and the *Sunday Post* (which has no equivalent anywhere). Across the top of eight of its nine columns it announced "Powerhouse Scotland". In small type it explained "Devolution . . . A Scottish Assembly — Here's What It Means Under Labour". The first five paragraphs were

15. *The Labour Party Manifesto for Scotland* (October 1974), p. 17.
16. *Ibid.*

30

unexceptional — though there was a nice touch in the third paragraph which commented that devolution was "too important to be left to the backroom wheeler-dealers in the other parties". The sixth paragraph, however, contained a phrase which later caused some trouble. In full it read:

> Unlike the Tory half-baked plan which simply means councillors attending a talking-shop, or the Liberal federal scheme which is alien to our democratic system, our plan means an Assembly *with economic teeth* (emphasis added HMD).[17]

The phrase carried a categorical promise which the Manifesto had avoided. Similarly the party political broadcast, implied by its tone a greater degree of devolution than the Manifesto promised. It was a discussion between Jim Sillars, Helen Liddell (then research officer of the STUC and now Scottish Secretary of the Labour Party) and George Foulkes (a prominent Edinburgh Councillor) and chaired by J. P. Mackintosh MP. Mackintosh, despite his eminent contribution to the devolution argument, was never a part of Sillars' group. Mackintosh (twice), Sillars (five times) and Foulkes (once) all spoke of Labour's promise to create a Scottish Parliament (subtly the word 'Parliament' promised more than 'Assembly'). Helen Liddell also said categorically that it would have control of the SDA.

The emphasis of both *Labour News* and the party political broadcast on October 7th was different from that of the Scottish Manifesto. The popular text promised things that the esoteric text did not. The SLP was later to make a great deal of these public promises. As we have seen their complaints were a little disingenuous since it was they who made the promises and exceeded their brief. For its part the Labour Party was careless. If it had been able to pay a full-time press officer, it could have demanded and ϧot more straightforward loyalty. As far as the broadcast was concerned no limits were imposed on what the participants could say, so they — not unreasonably — said what they thought. A party which puts so much ideological weight on its public promises should perhaps have been more careful.

IV

If the effect of the February election was to increase the leverage of the devolutionists within the Labour Party, the effect of the October election was even greater. Labour won 41 seats in Scotland on 36%

17. *Labour News*, October 1974, "Powerhouse Scotland", p. 2.

of the vote. The Nationalists displaced the Conservatives as second party (they got 30% and 24% of the votes respectively) with 11 seats. The Conservatives retained 16 seats and the Liberals 3. Perhaps more important, the Nationalists were now second to Labour in 35 of their 41 seats and well positioned to win a majority of the 71 Scottish seats at the next General Election. Sillars, however, won the largest majority (14,478) in Scotland. In the months after the election everyone in Scotland seemed convinced that the Government would have to push a devolution Bill through Parliament.

In the thirteen months between the election and the publication (much delayed) of the government's White Paper 'Our Changing Democracy' in November 1975 this conviction had three obvious results in Scotland. In the first place, devolution became and remained a major public issue. *The Scotsman*, the newspaper which took the greatest interest in the devolution battle, decided that devolution was a key story and often ran it on its front page. The other important sources of political news in Scotland, the BBC and STV, also made devolution an important news story. This had an effect on political journalists within Scotland for now there was a steady and increasing demand for their product. Their position grew stronger, their numbers increased and more journalists began to concentrate on political news in addition to their other interests. This led to competition between them for Scottish political news — and that could only be 'devolution'. Anyone, no matter how ill equipped, who would speak on the subject had a wide audience.[18] Nicholas Phillipson of Edinburgh University once described the dominant ideology of Scotland's quasi-nationalist agitators as 'noisy inactivity' Between October 1974 and November 1975 it became noisier.

This helped to create the impression that devolution was inevitable and began to raise questions about the changes it would bring. This was the second effect of the October 1974 Election. Within Sillars' 'mini-cadre' these thoughts led very shortly to a consideration of how and in what form the elections for Socialism should be fought in Scotland: in other words, it led to the formation of the SLP.

A third effect of the election, which reinforced the other two, was the suspicion that the Nationalists had cornered the market in 'Scottishness': that all the political advantage to be had from 'the

18. I know — I was one.

32

Scottish Dimension' would accrue to the SNP. Not surprisingly, this fear was felt in the Sillars' camp. It made them restive and irritable within the Labour Party. If the Labour Party was determined to go down with the anti-devolutionists, and its continued shufflings on the subject suggested it was, why should the devolutionists go too? On the other hand they could not, as Socialists, join the SNP. The same thought took another form: that there was need to ensure the continued existence of a *Socialist* party in Scotland. If the Labour Party, the argument ran, already weakened, was going to destroy itself on the rocks of 'the Scottish dimension', then there was need, even a duty, for its devolutionists to establish a separate party. Such a party could save Socialism in Scotland as Labour's sinking ship finally broke up. But, the devolutionists believed, it was necessary to hurry. They must leave the Labour Party before it destroyed itself; they must establish their credentials before the SNP gathered in Labour's increasingly disaffected voters. The race against the clock was about to begin.

A bare five weeks after the election the thinking of Sillars' group, including its last desperate attempt to save the Labour Party from itself, was telegraphed, publicly if pseudonymously. Bob Brown, former News Editor of the *Glasgow Herald*, published two articles under the *nom de plume* of "James Alexander" in his old paper on 25th and 26th November. These articles, the product of a year's reflection and discussions, gave an accurate prediction of what the Sillars' group was to do in the following year.

The first article, 'Labouring Along the Road to Devolution', is much the more interesting. The flavour of it is best captured if it is quoted at length:

Hard times and some bitter infighting lie ahead for the Scottish Council of the Labour Party, still bemused to find itself philosophically committed to the Scottish Assembly to which, until mid-summer, its leadership was so stubbornly opposed. . .

Next March 350 mandated delegates will arrive in Aberdeen's Beach Ballroom for the Scottish Council's 60th Annual Conference. They could turn out, in fact, to be travelling further along the road towards an independent Scottish Labour Party than the party managers meantime are prepared to admit.

The Government's Devolution Unit of Constitutional experts under the Lord President of the Council, Mr Edward Short, has made a start already on the complex task of preparing statutory legislation for the establishment of the Assembly.

33

Simultaneously the Labour Party's National Executive Committee have launched what seems likely to be the equally tough negotiations of reaching agreement with Scottish Socialists on the degree of policy-making and organisational autonomy which must also be devolved to Scotland from party HQ in Transport House.

At the Aberdeen Conference delegates will almost certainly be asked to vote on crucial resolutions — as fundamental as those on devolution itself which the Ayr Conference debated last March — calling for the creation either of a separate Scottish Labour Party or for far-reaching reforms to equip the Scottish Council with political bite while retaining some form of Transport House umbilical cord.

Labour's Scottish Council was inaugurated in 1915, its role (then as now) purely advisory. The Council, in sharp contrast to the Scottish TUC's muscle developed over 80 years, possesses little authority and minimum influence. Labour's activists recognise its incompetence to operate within an Assembly situation, in the new kind of political game that will be played henceforth in Scotland.

Comparisons are being made by some with the old Scottish Labour Party born in 1888 and pacemaker for the British Labour Party — and powerful enough in its own right to send its secretary, Keir Hardie, to the foundation Congress of the 2nd International in London and Paris in 1888-9.

This heady perspective of comprehensive autonomy is not regarded enthusiastically by the Transport House Mandarins. . . .

The MP for South Ayrshire, Mr James Sillars, leader of Labour's mini-cadre of hardline devolutionists who, in three years, has dented party complacency, has bluntly delineated what recent events presage. 'Policy-making in relation to a Scottish parliament,' he said, 'must be done in Scotland, not by the National Executive but by the Scottish element of the party; and for that the necessary policy-making machinery will be required. This means, *de facto*, a Scottish Labour Party.'[19]

"James Alexander" noted that the Labour Party was considering changing its organisation to accord with the new local government boundaries, and commented:

Three weeks ago the national organiser, Mr Reg Underhill, was in Glasgow. He made it plain that Transport House would crush like a cockroach any daft notions for a Scottish Labour Party, whatever fresh structure was devised.

SNP successes have provoked Labour's often petty hate-reaction as the party has been grudgingly propelled into a Scottish dimension. . . .

19. "James Alexander", Labouring Along the Road to Devolution, *Glasgow Herald*, 25.xi.74.

The SNP still control the game, forcing Labour to face the political reality of people's rising expectation of a Scottish parliament while squirming desperately to get away with its own teeny-bopper assembly responsible for strictly limited domestic functions. . . . Soon there will be other catalysts to endure . . . the Common Market Referendum. . . . It is whispered that nearly half of the (Scottish Parliamentary Labour group) are privately convinced that 'Yes' to the EEC will shift Scotland nearer to a sovereign parliament and direct Brussels representation. More importantly, it is also said that they are sure this would be right and proper.[20]

And that, of course, was the dominant tone. The Sillars mini-cadre was always sure that what they proposed to do was right and proper.

"James Alexander's" second article reiterated the ground of the first giving 'chapter and verse' of the maximalists frustration with the Labour Party, laying the blame on Westminster. The only new ground covered in the second article, 'Labour Must Give More Power to its Scottish Elbow'[21] was an elaborate plan for the constitution of the new Scottish Labour Party. This constitution, which bears some similarity to the eventual SLP Constitution, was clearly modelled on that of the SNP. It also afforded room for a much inflated party bureaucracy. A dozen paid officers and a secretariat were required. There should also be more full-time paid agents.

"James Alexander's" pieces were a blueprint for the new Scottish Labour Party: a party which was created a bare thirteen months after the "James Alexander" pieces appeared. But this is not to say that the move from plan to action was inevitable. For "James Alexander's" ideas were as much a dream as a blueprint. There was a good measure of wishful thinking behind the bluster and the threats to the Labour Party. Events in 1975 were to contrive to turn the wish to action.

20. *Ibid.*
21. "James Alexander" Labour Must Give More Power to its Scottish Elbow, *Glasgow Herald.* 26.xi.74.

Chapter III:

The Death or Glory Route

In 1975 there were three major incidents which combined to turn the dream of a return to the glorious days of the Scottish Labour Party (1888 version) into a reality. The first as "James Alexander" indicated was the 60th Annual Conference of the Scottish Council of the Labour Party in Aberdeen in March. By this time most of the Scottish press was aware of the existence of Sillars' group, but few thought much of it and nothing was said in print.

David Scott wrote in the *Scotsman* of March 21st:

> The most enthusiastic devolutionists in the party regard the Aberdeen Conference as probably the most important in the party's history.[1]

Three decisions had to be made at the conference which would affect the devolutionists' position. There was a resolution from Bute & North Ayrshire Constituency Party asking for semi-autonomy for the Scottish Council. There was a strongly worded resolution from the Transport and General Workers' Union (whose leader in Scotland, Mr Alex Kitson, had done much to make devolution official Labour Party policy) asking for an assembly "with economic teeth and revenue raising powers". Finally, Sillars was a candidate for a place on the Executive.

The Bute and North Ayrshire resolution was ruled 'out of order' by the Standing Orders Committee. A strong speech on its behalf by John Carson of Bute and North Ayr CLP was unavailing. So much for semi-autonomy. The composite resolution moved by the Transport and General urged the Government:

> (1) to ensure that the Assembly headed by an executive body, has a

1. *Scotsman* 21 March, 1975, p. 9.

guaranteed basis of finance and revenue raising powers. (2) to consider devolving to the Assembly, Department of Trade and Industry functions relating to the development of existing industry and attraction of new industry to Scotland. (3) to make the SDA answerable to the Assembly. (4) in conjunction with the Manpower Services Commission and the Training Services Agency, to develop further labour recruitment and training programmes consistent with the needs of existing and developing industry.[2]

Harry Ewing who was then Scottish Office Minister of State with responsibility for devolution, felt strongly enough about the subject to plead with Conference — in a minor breach of ministerial protocol — to make a definite decision on the composite. Deeply engaged in Whitehall tussles over the White Paper on devolution, he was in a good position to know that "this may be the final opportunity that the Labour Party in Scotland will have to make its position abundantly clear before legislation on devolution is published".[3] Sillars and J. P. Mackintosh spoke for; Norman Buchan (MP for Renfrewshire West) amongst others spoke against.

Despite expectations the T & G composite failed (by 353,000 to 341,000). Just why has always been a mystery. Certainly a number of trade unions had, even at that stage, not made up their minds on the subject. Their massive blocks of votes at Labour Party Conferences (each constituency party has 1,000 votes and each trade union a number based on claimed affiliations to the Labour Party — each of which is cast as a block) give effective power over conference decisions to the dozen largest affiliated unions. The leader of one union delegation told me that he was personally committed but not mandated by his union. In such cases speeches from the floor can make a considerable difference. He told me that the acrimonious tone of the debate between Mackintosh and Buchan, in particular, put up many delegates' backs. Mackintosh has recently pointed out that the Conference was more concerned with EEC membership than devolution. The Referendum was then only three months away. Mackintosh's speech was well enough received until, near the end, he likened the argument for devolution to the argument for Britain's being a member of the EEC: both were needed because Westminster was incapable of doing its job.[4] Did feeling against the EEC sway the vote? It is also widely believed by many who were there that the Boilermakers' Union could not be found in time to cast their pro-

2. *Ibid.*
3. *Ibid.*
4. Interviews with J. P. Mackintosh and Norman Buchan.

devolution block of votes. Whatever the reason the result was a set-back for the devolutionists which made the subsequent break of some of them all the easier. The immediate cause of their defeat — the absence of a well disposed union delegate — reinforced one of their objections to "Dalintober Street": trade union block votes were a curse. The SLP would do without them.

Although Sillars was elected on to the Executive, the main result was widely interpreted as a defeat for his group. The final paragraph of *The Scotsman's* leader on the Saturday morning (March 23rd) is an indication of this:

> One reason for this curious intransigence in the Labour Party is, of course, that many members hope to see a continuing centralisation of all economic power, with the eventual aim of transforming Britain into a wholly Socialist state. They presumably discount the possibility that the electorate will ever again do such curious things as returning a Tory government, which might be grateful for its power over a less Conservative assembly, let alone that it might return so many Nationalists that neither Unionist party could govern. They also discount the possibility that some staunch socialists might despair of their party, and put their hopes instead in an independent Scottish Labour Party, if not an independent Scotland.[5]

Evidently the *Scotsman's* leader writers were thinking along very similar lines to those pursued by the mini-cadre. More than this, the *Scotsman* was expressing itself in words very similar to those used by Sillars and his colleagues in *Scottish Labour and Devolution*. They had said:

> It would be an extremely foolish person indeed, who would count on never having a Tory administration governing in Scotland again.[6]

The *Scotsman* echoes the thought thus:

> They presumably discount the possibility that the electorate will ever again do such curious things as returning a Tory government, which might be grateful for its power over a less Conservative assembly. . . .[7]

But of course the most intriguing line in this leader is the suggestion that if the Labour Party does not stop behaving so perversely it will lose its devolutionists to an "independent Scottish Labour Party". Just this possibility had, as we have seen, crossed the minds of the Sillars mini-cadre. Was this suggestion in the *Scotsman* simply prescience? Or was it, perhaps, a signal from the *Scotsman* that it would be willing to give editorial encouragement to such a party if

5. *Scotsman* 23 March, 1975, p. 8.
6. Eadie et al., *Scottish Labour and Devolution*. p. 12.
7. *The Scotsman* 23rd March, 1975. p. 8.

anyone cared to create it? The sarcastic tone of the leader militates against the latter interpretation but it is impossible to dismiss altogether. Of course the creation of a new Scottish Labour Party, in competition with the existing Labour Party, was in line with *Scotsman* policy. It wanted to see a realignment of the parties and hoped that such a realignment would lead to a strong new centre party.

There was nothing improper about this policy. Newspapers have played at making and breaking governments before; why not parties? In Britain most of this manipulation of politicians and journalists by each other has taken place in London. But as Scotland comes to have a distinctive politics — with the approach of devolution (if not independence) — we must expect the same sort of things to happen here. When we look for reasons why the founders of the SLP had the courage to break from the Labour Party may we not weigh heavily the SLP's expectation of support from one of Scotland's leading sources of political news? Subsequent events in 1975 were to confirm the impression that the *Scotsman* was sympathetic to Jim Sillars personally and to his project of breaking up the Labour Party in particular.

II

The second incident in 1975 which spurred the SLP's planners on was the Referendum on EEC membership. The second Wilson government was unwilling, or unable, to reconcile its own belief that Britain should be a member of the Common Market with its party's strong, instinctively conservative rejection of it. Wilson had been opposed to the idea during the 1966 General Election. In the parliament which followed he had changed his mind but failed, as so often, to carry his party with him. His attempt to gain entry terms was rebuffed by the French. Perhaps they suspected the commitment of this new convert. The Heath government which followed suffered no such disability. Heath was a good 'European' of long standing. The terms of entry he hastily negotiated were accepted and Britain joined in 1972 without any test of popular opinion on the matter. The other three countries which considered joining at this time all had referenda. Heath's promise of a test of public opinion before entry was not honoured.

39

A coalition of political figures on the Right — Enoch Powell most effectively — and Left — virtually the whole trade union movement — opposed entry. Heath's move was applauded by most figures in the established centre of politics while many industrialists welcomed the opportunity to gain unfettered entry into a prosperous home market of more than 200 million people. The conflict between the powerful 'pros' and the many 'antis provided Wilson with an opportunity which few politicians could have resisted. He argued against the terms of entry — thus giving the impression he was against — while not committing himself to withdrawing if re-elected. His turn about proved useful in the 1974 General Elections as it provided Powell with a publicly acceptable excuse to campaign for Labour. Labour did unexpectedly well in the areas of England in which Powell is thought to have most influence.[8]

In the 1974 elections Labour was committed to renegotiating the terms of entry and to submitting the new terms to a test of public support either in a referendum or another General Election. The renegotiations took place and the government pronounced itself satisfied. Rather than risk yet another General Election it decided on a referendum which was called for June 5th 1975. To avoid embarrassing MPs, votes were not counted on a constituency basis. Instead, a regional basis was chosen after some dispute about whether all votes should be counted on a UK basis. Some were worried that Scotland and Wales might vote 'No' while England voted 'Yes' and that this result would be a gift to the Nationalist parties, who could then argue that their countries had been dragged unwillingly into the EEC by the English.

The decision to hold a referendum was taken by Wilson, partly at least to provide him with a democratic sanction for staying in the Market while not having to answer to his party for that decision. This could be achieved only if Labour Party people campaigned as individuals according to their consciences while the party machine remained out of the fight. This was a clever, short run, device to avoid a party split. That MPs might come to enjoy this freedom from party discipline so much as to weaken the hold of their parties in later contests, was discounted.

This is what happened in Scotland; at least in the 'anti' camp. Early in the campaign Sillars toured the country speaking on 'anti' platforms with Margo MacDonald, Senior Executive Vice-President

8. Johnson, R. W. and Douglas Schoen "The 'Powell Effect': or how one man can win". *New Society,* 22nd July, 1976, pp. 168-172.

of the SNP, and Teddy Taylor, the Conservative MP for Cathcart. The freedom from normal party disciplines enjoyed by all during this campaign also made it possible for the Sillars mini-cadre to operate more or less openly and to strengthen their ranks. The Market campaign and its immediate aftermath were heady experiences for the proto-SLP group which made the 'normal' constraints within the Labour Party all the more difficult to bear. And yet the Referendum campaign was not entirely satisfactory. After all, Sillars was on the losing side. Whether out of a dislike of being too closely associated with a failure, or because he was preparing his subsequent demarche Sillars appeared infrequently at the end of the campaign.

The *Scotsman* gave the Referendum campaign heavy coverage. Neal Ascherson, whose recent appointment as Scottish Political Correspondent, had been announced by the *Scotsman* on May 16th (". . . . Today we announce measures to consolidate our pre-eminence . . .") played an important role in this coverage.[9] That Ascherson, a man who had built an international reputation on the staff of the *Observer* should choose to return to Scotland at this point, was itself an indication of the news value now attached to Scottish politics. His employment by the *Scotsman* was a coup.

On May 31st the *Scotsman* carried an ORC poll showing 47% of Scots in favour of remaining in the EEC and 40% against. On June 2nd it reported the predictable decision of the SNP Annual Conference to urge a 'No' vote on the referendum. The *Scotsman* itself urged its readers to vote 'Yes' in a leader of 4th June. Also on that day it carried one in its series of articles in which both 'pro' and 'anti' views were put by members of the same party. J. P. Mackintosh was chosen to put the 'pro' view and Sillars to put the 'anti' view. Sillars used the occasion to put arguments which he was later to make familiar (and which the *Scotsman* was shortly to think sufficiently new and important to warrant front-page treatment). He argued that British membership would only strengthen the economic pre-eminence within Europe of the "Golden Triangle" bounded by The Ruhr, Milan and Paris. Scotland, Sillars urged, had learned hard lessons within the British 'common-market' about being on the periphery without sovereign institutions to protect her economy. In Europe her position, without separate representation, would be weak.

On the day of the referendum, June 5th, Ascherson reported that

9. *Scotsman* 16th May, 1975, p. 1.

41

the campaign had developed into an "auction of fear". He emphasised the Scottish aspect, "Unexpectedly rare were speeches which argued that Scotland — as opposed to Britain — would prosper more rapidly within the EEC". He went on to note that Harry Ewing and Sillars had developed the Scottish angle of the campaign towards the end, and commented:

> This timing, on the part of the men thought of as 'maximalists' on the devolution issue within the Labour Party, cannot have been accidental. We have probably been watching the building of a platform from which to launch a powerfully Scots-patriotic, if not nationalist political challenge after the results are declared. As one of Mr Sillars' critics in the party remarked: 'Jim is running for June the sixth — not the fifth'.[10]

That this report was 'probably' based on more than good guesswork hardly needs saying: why the knowledge that Sillars was building a base for a political challenge, knowledge which was common amongst Scottish political journalists (and not confined to Ascherson), was not pursued and reported as an important story in its own right is a complex question. Could it be that they sensed that Sillars had not yet decided definitely to 'go it alone' — and that a leak to the effect that he had, would be unfair. Or could it be that so many of these journalists were involved in building the challenge that they did not want to risk their project by a potentially damaging premature leak? It is impossible to say. But the fact that so many journalists were involved in creating a story they would some day report divided their loyalties.

Unaware of these moves Scots voted, though less overwhelmingly than the English, in favour of Common Market membership. Amongst Scottish regions only Shetland and the Western Isles voted against. Turnout in Scotland — 61% — was slightly lower than the 65% for the UK as a whole. 58% of Scots (UK 67%) voted 'Yes'; 42% of Scots (33% UK) 'No'.

The next day, the *Scotsman's* final summary of the Referendum campaign again put Sillars on the front page, this time preparing the way for his new line. Sillars was quoted as saying:

> It means that the Scottish people voted to stay inside the Common Market — no more, no less. There are no implications against devolution. I keep my belief that entry into the Common Market was not in our best interests. But it is now a closed matter, and we must think constructively about Scotland's role in the Common Market.[11]

10. *Scotsman* 5th June, 1975, p. 1.
11. *Scotsman* 6th June 1975, p. 1.

In a leader of Monday, June 9th, the *Scotsman* noted the SNP's difficulty. They had "associated themselves with a fairly comprehensive failure". So, of course, had Sillars.

Yet on that same day Sillars attempted to grasp the initiative. His attempt was reported as the leading story on the front page of the *Scotsman* on June 10th. The headline over the story was "Sillars Decides to Go It Alone". The report began:

> A Scottish nation-state, independent within the European Community. . . . After four years of preparation, Mr Jim Sillars MP, yesterday marched out on his crusade to convert the whole Scottish Labour movement to this faith.
>
> Mr Sillars . . . told a Glasgow Press Conference: 'This referendum does not close the question of Scotland's role in the EEC. It opens it up in another form. The Scottish people must make the choice between playing in the first division or the second'.
>
> Accepting the referendum verdict, Scotland must now struggle for independent representation in Community institutions — and Mr Sillars agreed (to a question by Ascherson) that this must also lead to *'a Scottish Labour Party as a distinct entity'.*
>
> A full country-wide campaign for this 'European independence' will be launched this autumn, and run through the winter until around March. Mr John Robertson, MP for Paisley, was the only ally Mr Sillars would name.
>
> In a six-page memorandum, based on the discussions of an unnamed group of colleagues, Mr Sillars states . . ." (emphasis added HMD).[12]

"James Alexander's" dream was coming true: The *Scotsman* noted:

> Mr Sillars who has been a leader of the anti-Market campaign.
> . . sets his time clock for Scottish independence within the EEC,
> and for a Scottish Labour Party taking its own place in the
> Socialist International, at about five to seven years.[13]

If Sillars was to continue making headlines, however, he would have to be attacked by others. Not for the last time the Scottish Council of the Labour Party obliged. The following day the *Scotsman* was able to quote Tom Fulton, Chairman of the Scottish Council of the Labour Party, who attacked the plan. Again the story was on page one: "Devolution Scheme is Sheer Arrogance". But later in the article it reported independent support for Sillars from a surprising quarter — the heart of the Scottish Council itself—

12. *Scotsman* 10th June, 1975, p. 1.
13. *Ibid.*

43

In a letter to 'The Scotsman' Mr Alex Neil says that "Sillars is articulating the views of a large and increasing number of Labour supporters and activists".[14]

In addition, the *Scotsman* carried a large front page story that the Scottish Parliamentary Labour Group had reacted so strongly to Sillars' memorandum as to invite him to set up his own party if he persisted in backing it. Neil's entire letter was printed on the letter page and the next day the *Scotsman* published the whole of Sillars' memorandum. Was the *Scotsman* making too much of a good thing? Perhaps. But it is worth saying that it had a lead on a major story and the prominence the paper gave to the story was a way of protecting this lead.

It is very easy now that the SLP has been founded and so much of the "James Alexander" argument put to use and acted on in the creation of the party to see what happened as the straight-forward unravelling of a conspiracy. Few political events work so remorselessly to the intention of their progenitors. To read such a smooth hatching of well laid plans into the creation of the SLP would be quite wrong. For one thing any such systematic behaviour requires a clarity of intention far beyond that which the SLP's creators possessed. There were signs as late as March 1976 — two months after the SLP's creation — that Sillars was still hoping his party could remain on amicable terms with the Labour Party. Sillars may not have been very realistic in this regard, but his position was always more ambiguous — and more flexible — than his public pronouncements suggested. For another thing we can see two hints, already in the *Scotsman's* reports of June, that things did not go entirely according to plan.

One hint was contained in the hope that a "full countrywide campaign" would be launched and continued until "around March". (Why March? — to coincide with the 1976 Scottish Council Congress?). Nothing of the sort happened. The SLP went public in December 1975. Another thing was the 'time clock' for independence and an SLP in the Socialist International in five to seven years. Again the plan was not allowed to mature. Outside events forced the pace.

The most important such outside event was, of course, the publication of the government's devolution White Paper "Our Changing Democracy". But before this, Sillars tried to prepare the ground for his break from the Labour Party by separating from his close friends Alex Eadie and Harry Ewing. The three had been living

14. *Scotsman* 11th June 1975, p. 1.

44

together when they were in London in a flat owned by Eadie's family. Early in October Sillars could take the strain of this proximity no longer. He told Ewing he was going to leave.[15] Ewing, afraid for his friend, insisted on leaving with Sillars; they moved to accommodation which Ewing secured in Marble Arch. No sooner were they settled, than Sillars told Ewing what was on his mind. He was going to leave the Labour Party and form a new party. In vain did Ewing attempt to dissuade him. Sillars was adamant. A new Scottish Labour Party which alone could meet the aspirations of the Scottish working class was inevitable. Someone was bound to seize the initiative. If members of the Labour Party did not make a move, perhaps someone in the SNP would break away to create the new party. The opportunity was there. Sillars would grasp it. The seeds sown by the mini-cadre and broadcast by 'James Alexander' were taking root in Jim Sillars' mind. Yet even so, he had some doubts. Should he abandon his base in the Labour Party? Was the time right? Whatever doubts there may have been in Sillars' mind about his ability to lead the new venture they can only have been allayed by Neal Ascherson's profile of him, "Jim Sillars: A future Prime Minister of Scotland?", which appeared in the *Weekend Scotsman* just when these arguments between Ewing and Sillars were developing — on November 1st. A modest man might have been emboldened by Ascherson's encomium:

> Even his enemies admit his ability, his eloquence, his flair for handling the media. Many colleagues wish he had accepted Harold Wilson's offer of a junior Minister's post at Health and Social Security last year. But Jim Sillars is one of the rare long-term thinkers in Scottish Labour, obstinate and passionate in his cause.

> Willie Ross may cut him in the corridors, but the fans at Wembley changed their chant to "Sillars, Sillars!" when they caught sight of him. A new Scotland is coming, and Jim Sillars, who doesn't like losing an argument and has gambled his political life on this one, will surely be one of its leaders.[16]

All that was needed now was an excuse.

15. Interview with Harry Ewing.
16. *Scotsman*, 1st November 1975.

The devolution White Paper, the third and final event in 1975 which completed the decision of the Sillars' group to form their own party, was that excuse. It was the publicly defensible cause of the party.

I was struck by the fact that, in my interviews with Sillars and his colleagues, none of them (with the possible exception of Litster Gardiner — a member of the SLP's Standing Orders Committee) seemed terribly concerned with devolution itself. They were much more concerned with how the Labour Party had handled — mishandled — the issue, and how this reflected on its ability to swim in the tempestuous tides and currents of Scottish politics. Secondarily, they were convinced that any devolved Assembly must have "economic teeth" to resuscitate the Scottish economy. Gardiner alone, and he belatedly, was concerned with the detail of the devolution settlement. The rest were horrified by the way the Labour Party appeared unable to take the initiative from the National Party. This was noticeably the focus of their reaction to 'Our Changing Democracy'.

They felt — still strongly feel — that the Labour Party in government had revealed itself unable to respond to the mood of the Scottish people and that the party had cynically played on Scots' strong desires for 'an Assembly with economic teeth' during the previous election campaign. (Let us leave aside the nice point about who made the promise.) If 'Our Changing Democracy' was the efficient cause of their rebellion; power over the Scottish Development Agency was the trip-wire within that document.

'An Assembly with economic teeth' was interpreted largely to mean, or at any rate thought to be impossible without, Assembly control over the SDA. The White Paper did not promise this control. Sillars told me — and his colleagues confirmed that he told them — that he had been led by Harry Ewing to believe that 'the SDA was in'[17] Ewing denies that he even spoke to Sillars about the White Paper.[18] Whatever reason Sillars had for believing that 'the SDA was in' he certainly campaigned for the White Paper. He told his South Ayrshire Constituency Party at their November meeting that they must all support the White Paper. He also campaigned for the government's plans on a tour of the Highlands in the weeks before

17. Interview with Jim Sillars.
18. Interview with Harry Ewing.

D

the White Paper was published.[19]

We now know that the White Paper, published on Thursday, November 27th, 1975, did not promise control over the SDA to the Assembly. What happened? Was Sillars misleading people to build up a case for rebellion? Was he being misled about it himself? If so, by whom? Or, did Sillars know all along what — in a general way — was in the White Paper; but. like the government itself, expect a good press for it? Certainly there was very little about the White Paper which was new or surprising. It would be useful to know the answers to these questions, but for the present purpose perhaps it doesn't matter a great deal. What does matter is that Sillars felt deeply betrayed — and this feeling spurred him on to create the SLP. He told me that Ewing had told him before publication that he had never lost a battle on the White Paper, and he observed — the remark conveys the mood — "I can only assume he never fought any."[20]

Sillars, and just about any other MP who was interested, saw the White Paper before it was officially published. Exceptionally, the White Paper was given by the government to the editors of Scottish papers forty-eight hours before publication. Government White Papers are commonly given to Lobby Correspondents (who can be trusted to keep their mouths shut) before publication so that their comment on them can be reasonably informed. But giving this White Paper to the Scottish press — itself an interesting indication of the government's recognition of the increasing power and importance of the press in Scotland — and giving it to them so long before publication, was an attempt to secure a good press for the government's proposals. The Scottish editors were not so circumspect as the Lobby Correspondents usually are. Sillars was told what was in it and so were many others. Sillars then (and others) knew not only what was in the White Paper but what the press reaction to it would be. He threatened, privately, to resign from politics altogether. Clearly the crisis had arrived. Neil and others dissuaded Sillars from resigning.[20]

If the government hoped by their generosity to the Scottish press, to get a good reaction, they were disappointed. In England the general reaction, particularly in the popular press, was that the White Paper offered too much and would lead to the break-up of the UK. In Scotland, the general reaction was that the proposals were 'not

19. Interview with Jim Sillars and Minute of South Ayrshire CLP of 15th November 1975.
20. Interview with Jim Sillars.

47

enough'. Some publishing groups had it both ways. The *Mirror* group's respective Scottish and English papers offered their respective Scottish and English audiences what they thought they would want to hear. The government might have felt it was being got at.[21]

Bob Brown, Sillars and Neil met in Sillars' home in Ayr the next day to consider what to do.[22] Their argument for breaking with the Labour Party at this point focused — in true left-wing Labour fashion — on the charge of 'broken promises'. It was on this basis that Sillars solicited support from other strong devolutionists such as J. P. Mackintosh.[23] The discussion between Brown, Sillars and Neil focused on the choices available to them at that moment. Staying in the Labour Party was never really seriously entertained by the proto-party for this would necessitate their forming an open formal group within the party and this they knew would never be accepted. Neil in particular felt that he could no longer stay in the Labour Party. A second possibility was considered: they could leave Labour as a group and join the SNP. This option couldn't be dismissed. But Sillars was strongly opposed because, he said, the SNP was not Socialist and he couldn't stomach the leaders of that party. A third possibility was that they should all abandon politics, but this was dismissed as defeatism. This left one option as "James Alexander" had presaged a year before. They could make the desperate gamble on forming an independent Labour Party. So it was agreed and pressed on the other members of the group. The main question then was how to make the decision public. Neil did not resign from his Labour party job at once. He and Brown, though not Sillars, continued to attend to Scottish Council business. Sillars and Robertson attended the regular monthly meeting of the Scottish Group of Labour MPs on December 2nd. At the meeting the White Paper was discussed. The meeting agreed that it "overwhelmingly supports the general proposals of the White paper on devolution". Sillars and, for different reasons, Tam Dalyell, (a strong anti-devolutionist) dissented but John Robertson did not.

Sillars insisted, when I talked to him, that the creation of the SLP was spontaneous; that it was not the result of a "Machiavellian plot"; that, indeed, "it was not Machiavellian enough".[24] There is some

21. Kellas, J. "Reactions to the Devolution White Paper" in Clarke, M. G. and Drucker, H. M. *Our Changing Scotland,* (Edinburgh, 1976), p. 70.
22. Interview with Bob Brown.
23. Interview with J. P. Mackintosh.
24. Interview with Jim Sillars.

truth in this. In the first place there are a number of very serious organisational questions which the founders of any new party must consider which in the emotion of the moment the founders of the SLP did not consider. There was, for example, hardly a moment's thought about how to deal with entrism from the extreme left. Secondly, it is "psychologically true" that the plan of breaking-away only definitely, irrevocably left the realm of "pub talk" to become a determined intention in the emotional aftermath of "Our Changing Democracy". But to suggest that the creation of the SLP was wholly spontaneous is to stretch credibility too far. It is to deny the existence of the mini-cadre.

IV

The first news of the SLP appeared on the *Scotsman's* front page in a story by Tom James, on December 10th. Tom James was a senior member of the *Scotsman's* parliamentary staff. The intimation that there was a story to be had if he could find and interview Sillars came to James by a circuitous route. On the morning of December 9th Ascherson rang Alex Neil in pursuit of a follow-up story on the devolution White Paper. Neil gave him the straight Labour Party reaction as was his job. But after he'd finished, Neil blurted out that he could not continue living a lie.[25] He was finished with the Labour Party. There was going to be a new party, Sillars was involved.

By itself this information was of limited use — it could justify a speculative feature but until Sillars confirmed it, was not hard news. Ascherson passed Neil's comments on to his Deputy Editor, Arnold Kemp. Kemp 'phoned James in London. James spoke to Sillars who, at first, denied he was forming a party. James was not so easily put down: was Sillars involved in forming a new party with others? Sillars gave James the story. James took a long time to 'phone his story back to Edinburgh. When he did it was a strong piece of hard news. The *Scotsman* ran the story on page 1. They had not only a fine scoop, but a news story of major importance, which signalled to many observers the possibility of large-scale defections from Labour. Perhaps it even presaged the break-up of the Labour Party.

James' story of the breakaway party, as it quickly became known, listed the three options which Neil, Brown and Sillars had discussed

25. *Scotsman* 12th December, 1975, p. 1.

and which are indeed familiar enough from "James Alexander". Sillars and his friends could (a) abandon politics, (b) join the SNP or (c) form an SLP. James reported:

> The breakaway movement appears to be small at the moment but it has representatives in virtually every layer of labour politics in Scotland.[26]

He then described the third option as "the political death or glory option", and noted "Mr Jim Sillars said he had no statement to make." No other names were mentioned.

The choice of the *Scotsman* as the vehicle in which to break the story of the SLP's creation was at once odd, and entirely explicable. The *Scotsman* was an odd choice because it has a largely Edinburgh based, middle-class readership. This is hardly the most fertile ground for the growth of a new Socialist party. On the other hand the *Scotsman*, in common with other "quality" newspapers, like the *Times* and the *Guardian*, devotes more space to political news than the popular papers. Moreover, the *Scotsman* had shown itself sympathetic to the Sillars camp on more than one occasion in the previous year, as we have seen. It thus had important advantages over other papers. Even popular papers with a working class readership and political staff, like the *Daily Record*, could not compete. The *Record* would not keep a political story on the front page as long as the *Scotsman*. The other possible competitor to the *Scotsman* was, of course, the *Glasgow Herald*. But the *Herald* had 'gone down market' after the removal of the *Scottish Daily Express'* printing and sub-editing to Manchester in March 1974. So the *Scotsman* was the best vehicle for the story. Once this decision had been made, it proved difficult for the *Glasgow Herald* to catch up. Its edition of December 10th carried a small anonymous inset on page one which simply noted that, "Dissatisfied Scottish Labour Party members are considering setting up a splinter group because of the government's White Paper on devolution". The next day it was little more informative. William Clark reported, on page 3, that:

> Mr James Sillars, a member of Labour's Scottish Executive and outspoken MP on devolution, yesterday denied he was spearheading a breakaway within the Labour Party in Scotland . . . "I am not leading any movement to a one-man party, a one-man band."[27]

Clark knew as well as anyone that there was more to the story than that, but Sillars stuck to his story. The *Herald* had little choice but to

26. *Scotsman* 10th December, 1975, p. 1.
27. *Glasgow Herald* 11th December, 1975, p. 3.

run the story as a matter of record. Thus was a pattern set which was repeated frequently during the initial hectic stages of the SLP story.

The new party was *Scotsman* front page news on December 11th, 12th and 13th. By this time the SLP was firmly entrenched as part of the devolution story. It was also part of the 'break up of the Labour Party' story. As the *Scotsman* had claimed pre-eminence on the devolution story only the previous month and was editorially committed to the rearrangement of the Scottish parties it was to be expected that it would try especially hard to maintain its lead on the SLP. It succeeded. It also got help. On the 12th of December, for instance, the paper reported "Sillars on the brink of Secession". He might join others in a new party. The story noted that Alex Neil's name was "identified with Mr Sillars' in the minds of supporters anxious to grapple with the SNP". It too used the now familiar formula of considering the options — though they had changed slightly in forty-eight hours. The options mentioned on the 12th were: 1. to stay in the Labour Party and fight; 2. "fight for autonomy for Scottish Labour within British Labour with Alex Kitson"; and 3.

Most extreme is the establishment of an independent Scottish Labour Party which would wake memories of the republicanism of Scottish Labour between the wars; stir the hearts of the old men; and perhaps offer a potent appeal to younger working class voters.[28]

Letting a story leak out a small fact at a time is a time-honoured way of keeping it in the headlines. A dozen leaks can sustain a story as one press conference cannnot. The technique was used to the full.

The period between the first leak — 10 December — and the Inaugural Meeting on January 18th was crucial for the SLP. In this period (counting the reporting of the meeting on the 18th in the papers of the 19th) there were thirty-two issues of the *Scotsman*. The SLP was on the paper's front page fourteen times: on December 10th, 11th, 12th, 13th, 17th (twice), 18th, 23rd, and January 7th, 10th, 12th, 13th, 16th and 19th. It was also a story on the inside pages fourteen times: on December 16th, 18th, 19th, 22nd, 23rd, and 31st and January 6th (twice), 8th, 12th, 15th, 16th, 17th and 19th. This is twenty-eight stories in thirty-two issues. The *Glasgow Herald* did its best to keep up. For the same thirty-two days it ran eleven front page stories and thirteen inside page stories.

However, by no means all of the stories were generated by the new party. The Labour Party did its flat-footed best to keep the story

28. *Scotsman* 12th December, 1975, p. 1

alive. Four of the *Scotsman's* stories were generated by the Labour Party's attempts to stop the rebellion. Another really striking thing about the reporting of the new party's creation is the thinness and occasionally the repetitiousness of the news reported. The news that Sillars was breaking from the old party appeared on the 10th of December. Then on the 12th it was "Sillars on the brink" and then again a week later "Sillars joins new Labour Party". Each time he made the front page. Good mileage was also made out of John Robertson's decision to join the new party. On December 17th it was "Another MP on the brink" and then on January 16th "John Robertson decides to join new party". Both stories were on the front page. The later report was the main story of the day. In the midst of this busy period it seemed that almost any story could be turned into an SLP story. On the 8th of January, for example, one of the of the *Scotsman's* two SLP stories was headed "no evidence of real split, Labour Claim". This was a story generated by a Labour Party Press Conference called to announce the Party's resolutions for its forthcoming Scottish Council meeting in March.

On its leader pages the *Scotsman* spelled out its attitude. It was not so much in favour of the new party as opposed to its opponents. On December 13th it asserted that it was sad that the Labour Party would close ranks against Sillars and Neil. What else they expected I cannot say. It further asserted in a Leader on December 23rd that the Labour Party had split over devolution and hoped that the Conservative Party might do so as well. The Conservatives did not oblige. The *Herald* on the other hand was much more sceptical of the SLP. It feared the new party was too left-wing.

The full implications of the relationship between the Scottish political press in general, the *Scotsman* in particular and the SLP are too complicated to be considered fully here. I will return to the subject in my final chapter. For the present it is sufficient to note that the prominence given by the *Scotsman*, and to a lesser extent, by other Scottish papers was a considerable boon to its recently politicised staff. Here at last was a purely political story which was about Scotland (and unlike the Chrysler story) breaking in Scotland. With twenty-eight stories about the SLP in thirty-two days, it cannot be denied their opportunity was grasped to the full. On the other side the founders of the SLP needed the press even more than it needed them. A great blaze of publicity was a precondition of a successful launching of their party. Socialists do not expect, and do not normally get a good press. Yet they crave good publicity. The fact that

Sillars' revolt was being taken so seriously by the press was a considerable factor in attracting people out of the Labour party and into the SLP. The fact that this publicity was so well orchestrated — the SLP was on the front page of the *Scotsman* on Monday, Tuesday and Friday of the week before the all important Inaugural Meeting —only helped the more.

Chapter IV:

The New Beginning

The Machiavelli whose precepts the leader of the SLP regrets not having followed was not a Prince. He was a Secretary to Princes. In this respect he resembles Alex Neil, the General Secretary of the SLP, more than Sillars himself. Much of Machiavelli's teaching concerns beginnings. He urged would-be Princes, as well as founders of Republics, to take great care over their first steps, for these would do much to determine what came later. Well might Sillars have heeded that advice, for much of the character of the SLP was determined by its first steps.

Between November 27th and the SLP's inaugural meeting what was required was the transformation of the 'mini-cadre' into a public nucleus of the new party; the formation of the bare outlines of a working constitution which this group could operate; the articulation of a basic ideology to attract members and define a political space for the new party, distinct from both Labour and National parties; the establishment of key branches around Scotland; the choice of officers; the planning and organisation of the inaugural meeting and the constant stimulation of the Press.

This can be put more simply: having decided to abandon his political base Sillars had to act quickly to create another. The first step in this process occurred at the regular monthly meeting, on December 21st, of The General Management Committee (G.M.C.) of the South Ayrshire Constituency Labour Party. Before this meeting Sillars made literally no attempt to carry his G.M.C. with him. He did not discuss the existence of his private group with them.

He made no attempt to soften the blow to the group or even to carry a section of the party machine with him.[1] Such an attempt need not have been as futile as it may now seem. The South Ayrshire G.M.C. had a proud tradition, in much less tolerant times, of supporting rebellion. It always backed Emrys Hughes in his fights with Labour's leadership. Moreover, a great many of the G.M.C. were intensely loyal to Sillars personally. Some at least, perhaps even some entire branches, might have followed him had he prepared the ground better. Their subsequent bitterness about Sillars' rebellion owes not a little to the way he "betrayed" them just as Sam Purdie had done before.

If the South Ayrshire Party were an ordinary Constituency Party, or if South Ayrshire were a normal inner-city Labour stronghold, Sillars' attitude might not be too difficult to understand. But neither the seat nor the Labour Party in it is anything like normal. South Ayrshire is well nigh impossible to organise without an extremely efficient machine. It consists of a series of villages, many of them mining or former mining villages strung out with various small centres (the G.M.C. actually meets in Ayr — outside the Constituency), over a large tract of South Western Scotland. Even the National Party with its legendary plethora of local branches finds the seat difficult to organise. On the other hand, this seat had produced the largest Labour majority in Scotland in October 1974. On top of that, the South Ayrshire Labour Party which had so successfully fought the seat was no ordinary run down Constituency party. On the contrary it had 1,800 paid-up (not social) members, a full time agent, a car and committee rooms of its own.

Since the SLP is so largely dependent on Sillars, and Sillars' power is so heavily dependent on his being an MP, his decision to abandon his Constituency and leave it intact to be used against him in future elections was a step of singular political bravery if not suicide. But it was also more than that.

It was an important part of the rejection of the old machine politics. Sillars and his colleagues did not see themselves simply setting out to create a rival Labour Party. They were attempting to create a new kind of Socialist Party altogether. Their quarrel with the Labour Party was not fundamentally about devolution. Devolution was simply the efficient cause of their leaving behind a party whose very organisation had come to stink in their nostrils. What they

1. Interview with Jim Sillars April 1977: and Jim Tanner June 1977.

55

wanted was to get away from the mechanism of party-organisation as it is known to the Labour Party. They wanted to be rid of the 'Tammany Hall' aspect of the Labour Party with its jobbery with trade union block votes.

That is why "Dalintober Street" infuriated them. They 'won' a vote there in favour of devolution and were thus indebted to a kind of jiggery-pokery they detested. Their new party would have no trade union block votes. That was decided early on. In place of a party built on block votes and constituency committees, the SLP would attempt to be a party based, as purely as possible, on an idea. It would break out of the mould of the Labour Party and, led by the charismatic Sillars, would call on the deep reservoir of Scottish socialism. He would—with support from the Press—build up a membership of like minded people who had also been pried loose from the old party system by a combination of Labour's ineptness and the National Party's example.

The SLP would be an ideological party. I have said that this was to be a new kind of party. That is not quite right. The original Labour Party had been such a party. But sometime in the early years of its history it had lost its way. The SLP would revive the halcyon days of Labour's youth. In the Scotland which Sillars and his colleagues saw emerging, it would be possible to build a party which would do without the 'machine' of the Labour Party. Instead, Sillars would build a campaigning party with a new base. It would be a cross between an American Presidential campaign and a CND crusade. It would not be at all like the sordid boring Labour machine politics they had left behind.

Their first step was to draft a 'shadow' constitution. This was done by Sillars, Neil and John Robertson in the MPs' room in Westminster soon after the White Paper was published. The party would have a democratic Constitution. Voting would be by individual membership in branches based on residence and place of work. Branches would affiliate to a national party without going through Parliamentary organisations. But despite its democratic Constitution, the party was founded on a contradiction. On the one hand the notion of a truly democratic party was well judged to attract hundreds of intelligent hard working activists. Many of them were fed up with the Labour Party precisely because it was not 'democratic'. And yet its attempts to create a democratic structure could not disguise the fundamental truth about the SLP: it was Sillars' organisation. It could disagree with him only with his

56

permission. If need be Sillars could threaten to resign. In extremis as at the party's first Congress this is what happened and when Sillars threatened to resign everyone else backed down — or left, or was expelled. In other words there was a fundamental contradiction in the SLP between its democratic ideology and the actual distribution of power. But the truth of this contradiction was not evident at first.

The second step in the establishment of the SLP was the transformation of the 'mini-cadre' into a public working proto-organisation which could organise the Inaugural Conference. This was accomplished at a meeting on December 23rd in the Ingram Hotel, Glasgow. Here Bob Brown was chosen first Chairman of the party. Don Robertson became Vice-Chairman; Alex Neil became Acting-Secretary and a small Organising Committee was formed. Sillars did not attend this meeting. The line was that the meeting was to organise itself as the Scottish Labour Party and then 'invite' Sillars to join. In this way the notion that the party was not 'a one-man band' would be maintained. This was a harmless conceit; but a conceit it was. Sillars drove David McMurran, an old acquaintance from Auchinleck to the meeting. McMurran, who was an AUEW shop-steward at Scottish Aviation, was to become the party's Industrial Organiser. At the Ingram meeting he became part of the Organising Committee.[2] All the old 'mini-cadre' were there. In addition to Brown and Neil, Jimmy Frame and Jim Fyfe joined the Organising Committee. New blood in addition to McMurran and Don Robertson included Jim McCaffrey, a Labour councillor from Tillicoultry. At least some journalists who did not join the Organising Committee, among them Neal Ascherson and Ruth Wishart *(Daily Record),* were at the meeting. Others waited outside for the news.

The early recruits to the party came from several directions. A good many were friends and acquaintances of Sillars and Neil. Loyalty to them explains some otherwise surprisingly large branches. Neil's home town of Patna (which has fewer than 2,000 voters on its electoral register) produced a branch of seventy members — the SLP's largest. In Ayr, the home of Sillars and John Robertson, there were 54 members in the branch. In fact more than a third of the party came from Ayrshire.

Recruits also came as a result of Sillars' and Neil's speaking engagements in the period before the Inaugural Meeting. St. Andrews and Cumbernauld branches were, amongst others, formed

2. Interview with David McMurran.

in this way. The St. Andrews' case is illuminating. Don Robertson now a lecturer at Stevenson College in Edinburgh and then Secretary of the East Fife Constituency Labour Party, wrote to Sillars in June after reading in the *Scotsman* Sillars' ideas on Europe. He asked him to address a public meeting in St. Andrews. Sillars agreed. The meeting, held in mid-December, was an electric occasion: it was the largest Socialist meeting in St. Andrews Robertson could remember. After the meeting he told Sillars how impressed he was with what the SLP was doing. Sillars thereupon invited Robertson, whom he had never previously met, to the Ingram Hotel meeting on December 23rd at which plans for the public inaugural meeting were to be laid. At the Glasgow meeting Robertson was made Vice-Chairman of the Party.[3]

Other recruits heard about the Party from the Press, were attracted by its political line, and went as individuals to the inaugural meeting. Some of them, like Jim Young (a history lecturer at Stirling University) were later themselves to form branches. He and McCaffrey created the Tillicoultry branch (11 members); and Young had a formative role in the creation of the Stirling University branch (10 members).

Other recruits came from the Scottish Aggregate of the International Marxist Group (IMG). The IMG welcomed the formation of the SLP as the beginning of what some of them believed would be the break-up of the monolithic British Labour Party. They welcomed the new party in the January 22nd issue of *Red Weekly* and went in some strength to the Inaugural Meeting where they declared their intention of joining.[4]

While the party was acquiring supporters by this mixture of friendship and idealism, plans had to be made for the Inaugural Meeting and the bare bones of the party's programme established. The Inaugural Meeting was scheduled for Sunday afternoon, January 18th, in the Grosvenor Hotel, Glasgow. The timing was deliberate: January 18th was the day on which the Labour Party in Scotland was to launch its campaign 'Devolution not Separation' to promote the White Paper. Ironically, the Scottish Council had agreed to this campaign on the prompting of Sillars and Neil and the choice of date had been theirs. By having the SLP inaugural meeting on the same day that Labour's campaign opened, the SLP hoped to steal a march on the Labour Party, for the Press could be depended

3. Interview with Don Robertson.
4. James, Alan and McAllister, James, "The Scottish Labour Party", *Red Weekly*, 22nd January 1976, p. 5.

on to compare the attendance at the various meetings.

The SLP's ideology, as enunciated by Sillars and Neil in their speeches in this period, had a number of strands. The SLP was to be more Scottish than the Labour Party and more Socialist than either that party or the National Party. It would dispute Labour's claim to have inherited the mantle of Scottish Socialism: of Keir Hardie and Tom Johnston. This dispute would be raised on the SLP's side by its emphasis on the need for more jobs — especially skilled industrial jobs — to be brought to Scotland. The failures of successive Labour Governments in this respect were repeatedly emphasised. In addition the party's advocacy of its 'Scotland in Europe' line on the Constitutional question would make it more Scottish than Labour. Its leaders talked increasingly of a Scottish Parliament.

'Scotland in Europe' — the slogan was barely developed beyond Sillars' Memorandum of June 1975 — became the key to the SLP's ideology in another way for it served to distinguish the new party from the National Party. After the June '75 referendum, the SNP leadership covered its internal differences — and kept its options open — by seeking refuge in the 'Second Referendum' formula on European Common Market membership. When Scottish independence had been achieved voters would be given another chance to say if they — this time as Scots — wanted to remain in the Community. This question-begging formula left room for Sillars to advance his 'Scotland in Europe' slogan as a distinctive position. Another advantage of Sillars' formula was that it allowed him to be very keen on "the Scottish Question" — urging independence in fact — without risking the accusation of "Separatism". He didn't want separation from anyone. Equipped with this formula he could dispute the National Party's claim to be the sole representative of 'Scotland'.

To this battle on two fronts — to seize 'Socialism' from Labour and 'Scotland' from the SNP — Sillars added the claim that the SLP would be a democratic party. From my interviews with SLP members it seems that all three elements attracted members. But the attraction of the 'democratic' element was much more powerful than Sillars' emphasis on the other two suggests that he realised. This was eventually to lead to great disenchantment.

It is also evident that Sillars was out of touch with Scottish left wing thinking on Europe. In Scotland the Left were opposed to Europe. Since the referendum this opinion had hardened. Sillars' hasty combination of 'Socialist' and 'European' elements led to trouble because he thus committed himself to a line which few were likely to follow. This problem was soon perceived by Sillars' enemies in the party both inside and outside the IMG. It gave them a 'Socialist' card to play against him which could not be dubbed 'extreme left-wing'.

An indication of just how 'ideological' the party was, and how relatively unimportant its leaders thought organisational questions, is given by their attitude to "dual-membership". In the early hectic days before the Grosvenor Hotel Inaugural Meeting the idea of excluding left wing entrists never occurred to them. When they spoke of "dual-membership", as they often did in this period, the duality they had in mind was between the SLP and the Labour Party. This duality they welcomed in order to make the Labour leadership face the opprobrium of excommunicating SLP members — rather than the other way round. This was an old Communist Party line: force them to throw you out. As former Labour Party members they knew Labour would tolerate almost any splinter group until that group put up candidates against Labour candidates. This the SLP would eventually do but there was no need to hurry the break. Indeed, Sillars was to assure his National Organising Committee in February and March that he was on the best of terms with Bob Mellish (the Government Chief Whip) and had an agreement not to resign the Labour whip until the Dock Work Regulation and Shipbuilding and Aircraft Industry Nationalisation Bills were safely through parliament. With their eyes firmly fixed on this aspect of dual-membership no thought was given by the SLP's founders to IMG or other Trotskyist infiltration.

Two other points about the hectic cobbling together of the party — and particularly of its ideology — should be noticed here. The very *ad hoc* and ill-considered expression of the ideology actually attracted members. So far from appearing cynical, this obviously incomplete series of slogans attracted a small number of the most intelligent political thinkers in Scotland. Its very incompleteness suggested the possibility of joining and working towards a more comprehensive, more 'class-conscious' ideology. Tom Nairn, Bob Tait, and Jim Young, all prominent members of the party joined partly for this reason.[5] Whether they and others like them could have agreed on any specific ideology is open to question: but that question did not arise at first. What mattered was that they saw hope in Sillars'

5. Interviews with Tom Nairn, Bob Tait and Jim Young.

60

position. Again this was an immediate advantage — respected people joined — but one which did not last.

It should be noted that by building his party on the basis of ideological affinity, Sillars inevitably created an intellectuals' party. Those trade union leaders who were strong devolutionists like Alex Kitson (of the TGWU) were not brought in. It was never likely that they would be. The Labour party gives trade union leaders too much power for them to be easily tempted by a new competing party. They are also wary of any organisation which might split the votes of their members. Furthermore the SLP did not bring in a single branch of the old Labour Party. The new party thus failed to attract any organised support from the working class of Scotland. Instead it drew individuals, people who — whatever their background — were prepared to act outside conventional working class organisations. Thus, from the beginning there was a contradiction between the party's actual membership (the Ayrshire group aside) and those it hoped to attract. To be a working-class socialist party the SLP needed to attract skilled and unskilled manual workers. In fact it was dominated perhaps even more than the Labour party is by teachers, journalists, students, social workers and academics. A study by Stuart Hood, an Aberdeen University student, of the Aberdeen branch illustrates this point. Hood found that nearly three-quarters of the fifty people who were or had been members of the branch in the Spring of 1977, were less than 35 years old. Only 15% had manual occupations (Registrar-General's category IIIm) while 31% were students. There were no unskilled manual workers. Whereas 8% of the British population has been educated at University, 53% of the Aberdeen branch had reached that level and another 11% were or had been post-graduates.[6]

Thus gathered, the party moved to its Inaugural Meeting on January 18th. Those who arrived were asked to join the party at the door and pay its £2 membership fee. Many paid up, but those who baulked were allowed in for a lesser amount. The meeting was not precisely either a public meeting or a private restricted affair. News of its time and place were passed around by letter and word of mouth. There was none of the poster campaigning or leafletting which normally preceeds a public meeting of a left-wing party nor was the press informed of the time or place. This 'semi-private' form was a

6. Hood, Stuart. *The Scottish Labour Party and Survey of Aberdeen Branch* (typescript available from the Politics Department of the University of Aberdeen). Section vii.

stroke of genius. It ensured that anyone who was remotely aware of what was happening would be there. The incentive to find out was increased by the lack of public information. More important it ensured that everyone who turned up had a sense of participating in the meeting in a way which a merely public gathering could never have achieved. About four-hundred people attended. It was a day of sheer magic. The centre piece speech was, of course, Sillars'. He did not disappoint his supporters' expectations. Jim Young told me, and more to the point, told Sillars at the time, that it was the best Socialist speech since Nye Bevan's death. Much of the speech was about devolution. It demanded "a strong Scottish parliament working within the broad framework of the United Kingdom". But it was about much more as well. Its audience, even those who are now thoroughly disenchanted with Sillars, can repeat some of its phrases at the slightest prompting. Sillars called on all the themes of the Left. He appealed to those who were fed up with the old Labour Party; to those who had left it over its support for the American war in Vietnam. He insisted that his new party would be democratic: "Join Us and Make Us", he said. It was the right speech for the occasion. It brought in support for the party across the spectrum of the Scottish left-wing. Many of those who went to the meeting out of curiosity were delighted by what they heard. It is doubtful if many of these people would have joined a 'devolution' party. Sillars broadening of his appeal "We are not a one-man band, not a one issue party" was highly successful. This broadening was particularly important in bringing in important members of IMG in Scotland and key members of what was to become the SLP's Kelvin branch.

A cyclostyled sheet "The Scottish Labour Party: Statement of Aims" emphasised the shortcomings of the old Labour party and stated that the SLP proposed to overcome these failings. It proposed a remit for an Organising Committee. (see Appendix A)

That Committee, the National Organising Committee (NOC), as it came to be called was created at the Inaugural Meeting. The people present agreed, without dissent, to put all the members of the "Steering Committee" — the Ingram Hotel group — onto the NOC. At the suggestion of Don Robertson, who had become chairman, they added people 'from the floor'. These were John Nairn of Cumbernauld who was nominated by his eight strong group from Cumbernauld, Ron Kerr of Newbattle Abbey College, Mrs Margaret Mellis, a long-time Socialist from Fife and Hugh Gray

62

from Edinburgh. The last two nominated each other. Gray was sitting in front of Mellis. He turned to her and said "You nominate me and I'll nominate you". Barbara Reid of Stewarton was also nominated at this time. Unfortunately for them, the IMG members there lacked the presence of mind to shout one of their members on. Other members were co-opted later.

The meeting received the favourable publicity for which its organisers hoped. The coincidence of an SNP victory in a local government by-election in East Kilbride enabled *The Economist's* anonymous correspondent to underline Sillars' speech in his report of the Conference:

> For the government the signs are at last overwhelming that, whatever the perils of the English backlash, Scottish voters are asking for a Scottish Assembly with a much more powerful devolved authority than the White Paper contemplates.[7]

II

The central question about any organisation is 'Who rules?'. In the case of the SLP there was never any doubt: the organisation was formed from the top, around the dynamic personality of Jim Sillars and his friends, and formed down. Sillars' position as a well known and articulate MP together with his action in leading his small cabal for five years before the public break with the Labour Party served to ensure his absolute dominance. He used this position to the full. It is, indeed, a tribute to his charm and the success with which he tapped the considerable discontent with the Labour Party, that this central dominance was not obvious from the beginning.

Formally the central organisation was the NOC. In fact the NOC consisted of various loosely organised groups. Sillars and Neil were close throughout. Bob Brown, Don Robertson and Jim Fyfe aided, occasionally, by Joe Farrell were an informal second tier. Don Robertson told me that Neil and Sillars were disconcerted by the way the four additional members were added to their hand picked Steering Committee when it became the NOC.[8] The NOC was therefore thought to be uncontrollable and was not trusted by Sillars, Neil and Don Robertson. The practice of plotting against Executive Committees had become a habit in 1971-75. It was not a source of strength. The other MP in the party, John Robertson did not play a

7. "Labour has to decide on ousting" *Economist* 24th January, 1976. p. 25.
8. Interview with Don Robertson.

major role. He attended no Executive Meetings before June 1977 and was, indeed, given a London address on the NOC mailing list. Robertson was not a notably active or outspoken MP either before or after he joined the SLP.

The leaders' anxiety to retain control became one part of the argument about admitting new members. The possibility of Jimmy Reid joining the party was discussed privately before the second NOC meeting on February 28th by Alex Neil and some NOC members. Reid, who had recently left the Communist party and was a man of considerable authority because of his struggle to keep Upper Clyde Shipbuilders open, was the kind of recruit the SLP needed. He could have helped the party in the Engineering Section of the AUEW and would have added much to its credibility in that industry. Among those who reacted favourably to this approach were Don Robertson, John Nairn, then Secretary of the Cumbernauld branch, and David McMurran, then a Shop steward at Scottish Aviation's South Ayrshire plant and Industrial Organiser of the SLP. The leaders were opposed for two reasons: they feared the taint of Reid's recent association with the Communist Party, and they doubted he could be controlled. Jim Young, then also on the NOC, remembers Sillars — jokingly? — saying "If we have that man in the party he'll be competing with me for time on the box".[9] McMurran told Reid later that it was agreed that he could join after a year's lapse of his C.P. membership.[10] Eighteen months later Reid joined the Labour Party.

At the first NOC meeting another important matter was discussed. Harry Ewing had that morning been reported in the *Glasgow Herald* (but not the *Scotsman)* as saying that the SLP was facing a stormy time unless it did something about its IMG members[11] The NOC immediately decided — it was their very first decision — to rule out dual membership with parties other than the Labour Party. The party wanted to keep the bridges back into the Labour Party open — Sillars and John Robertson did not even resign the Labour Parliamentary Whip until July — and, as we have seen, it suited them to make the Labour Party go to the trouble of throwing them out rather than simply leaving. But the other parties were declared anathema. The 'dual-membership' rule, as it came to

9. Interview with Jim Young.
10. Interview with David McMurran. Reid, while not unsympathetic to the SLP's intentions, never considered joining seriously. Interview with Jimmy Reid.
11. *Glasgow Herald*, 24th January, 1976, p. 5.

be called was the SLP's answer to Ewing's warning.[12]

Another paramount concern of the NOC was the establishment of branches. Branches, and an active membership, would be useful in a number of ways — regardless of their role in the party's decision making procedures. They could establish the party's presence across the country; raise money for themselves and the centre; distribute leaflets with a view to gaining more members and fight local government and General Elections. All these matters were discussed, on a report of the Secretary at that same meeting.

Neil reported that the general pattern would be for existing members (as of the Grosvenor Hotel) to meet, elect a committee, and run a recruitment campaign. The NOC decided to hold a meeting in May at Middleton Hall (South of Edinburgh) of all branch Secretaries and Chairmen. It was also decided that Bob Brown would circulate the branches with a 'specimen' letter which they could try to have published in the local paper. Branches would be affiliated to the NOC and recognised by it.

From the first the party was operating on two levels: the branches and the NOC. There was little attempt to co-ordinate the branches or to give them anything to do, save to build their own organisations. Some activity, indeed, almost any activity — such as local canvassing, a campaign of marches against the cuts in government spending or the drafting of policy proposals — almost *any* activity would have been a tonic for it would have shown doubters that the SLP stood for something and would have transformed its membership into a fighting force. Yet having built a campaigning party Sillars and Neil campaigned very little: a General Election would have transformed the party, and to be fair, Sillars was constantly warning his party that a General Election was imminent. But it didn't come in time. Thus the party was left largely to its own devices and the truth of Machiavelli's dictum was borne out: the pattern of the first steps proved impossible to change.

Nevertheless, the party grew quickly. It came to have just short of nine hundred members by the October conference. Though the leaders made a practice of issuing fallacious statements which exaggerated the membership — 2,000 members were often claimed — this should not obscure their real achievement in getting the nine hundred [13] (see Appendix B). Among them were a fair number of energetic and politically intelligent activists: most of them young. Sillars and his friends were not alone in making for a new political

12. Minute of NOC Meeting 24th January, 1976.
13. See, for example, Ascherson, N., "Scotland's Socialist Schismatics" *Scotsman*, 27th February, 1976, p. 11.

home, untainted by compromises of the Labour Party and more Socialist than the National Party. Had they succeeded in welding their supporters into a coherent party they could have been a force.

Yet from the beginning, the formation of branches raised problems. The greatest of these problems arose in Glasgow. The first meeting of the Glasgow members occurred on February 12th. They met in response to a letter from three of their number, Matt McClure (who was on the NOC), Joe Farrell (who was to be co-opted onto the NOC at its February meeting) and Bill Copeland. The letter was dated 4th February, and informed the Glasgow members that "it is now time to establish a branch in Glasgow, so that organisation here does not lag behind that in other parts of the country".[14] The sixty-seven people who attended elected a Branch Committee. The IMG members at the meeting — four by my count — declared their presence. This was noted by the NOC.

The position of the Glasgow branch became crucial immediately after its first meeting partly because some of its members had declared themselves to be members of the IMG despite the dual-membership rule, and partly because there was to be an election in Darnley for a seat on the Glasgow District Council. Darnley is in the part of South-West Glasgow which is included in Pollok constituency. The sitting Councillor had been jailed on a petty corruption charge. The seat was ripe for an SLP challenge: a challenge which would keep the party in the news, give its members something to campaign about and, if successful, enable it to keep the initiative. A Special Meeting of the NOC was called for March 13th to consider the matter of Darnley.

The NOC agreed to fight the seat. It had little choice. As Stewart MacLachlan (a Glasgow SLP member) had put it in his *Daily Record* column the previous day:

> The SLP will contest any parliamentary election in Scotland, and since not many of these can be expected over the next few months it will also fight the first suitable local election. "Suitable" means that it has to be in the Strathclyde area — the Darnley district election in Glasgow, caused by the jailing of Councillor Gordon Kane, is a possible — because the party does not yet feel it has found the strength to challenge outside the West of Scotland.[15]

But, if, on the one hand, the NOC saw the logic of its position as MacLachlan had explained it, it also had a delicate problem with its

14. Farrell, J., Letter of 4th February, 1976.
15. MacLachlan, S., *Daily Record* 12th March, 1976.

Glasgow branch. They — not the NOC — ought to be deciding whether or not to fight the seat, and if so, how to organise themselves to fight it. Joe Farrell (Glasgow's Chairman) informed the NOC meeting that the IMG members in the Glasgow branch might prove difficult. On the other hand, there were enough SLP members in Pollok Constituency for them to form a branch there. This hived-off branch would not be troubled by IMG members. The NOC was also influenced by the possibility that there would also be a by-election in the Ruchill/Milton seat on Strathclyde Regional Council. The Labour Councillor in this North Glasgow seat was threatening to resign. It would be important for the NOC to prevent the IMG from controlling the choice of the SLP's candidate in this seat.

The special NOC of March 13th considered asking the Glasgow Branch to set up a Pollok Branch. The Minute of the meeting is ambiguous about just what was decided. On the one hand, it clearly says that they should "Consult Glasgow Branch re setting up Pollok Branch". But the next sentence says that "only members from Pollok could nominate candidates", and the sentence after that speaks of the "Pollok office-bearers".[16] The NOC definitely decided to fight Darnley regardless of the opinions of the north Glasgow members, no matter how they were organised. Farrell wrote on March 15th to all members inviting them to an emergency meeting of the Glasgow Branch on the following Thursday — the 18th. The letter regretted the shortness of the notice:

> . . . but the matter which will have to be considered is of great importance to the future of the SLP. The meeting will be asked to consider the importance of establishing area branches within Glasgow to provide a better opportunity for more widespread participation by the party members not able easily to attend meetings in the centre of the city.
>
> In addition as the SLP will have to consider contesting local by-elections including the one about to take place in the Darnley district, it is vital that the most democratic machinery exists within the party at grass roots level. There are a number of areas where we already have a sufficient membership to form local branches, including the Pollok area where Darnley is situated.[17]

In other words, the NOC had panicked at the presence of a handful of IMG members in its Glasgow Branch. It decided to fight Darnley, but to pretend to the Glasgow membership that the Branch would be

16. Minute of NOC Meeting 13th March, 1976, p. 1.
17. Farrell, J., Letter of 15th March, 1976.

deciding on whether or not to fight the seat.

The Glasgow Branch Committee met immediately before the full meeting. Alerted by loose talk from NOC members in pubs, as well as Stewart MacLachlan's column of March 12th, the Committee was in no mood to take dictation from the NOC.[18] Neither was it happy about the decision of Don Robertson and Alex Neil to come to the meeting and demand to speak to the membership from the platform. The Branch Committee voted to consult the full Branch on all the relevant matters. When the full Branch was convened it supported it s Committee's decision against the insistence of Joe Farrell. In particular, Farrell wanted Robertson and Neil to be allowed to speak from the platform. The Branch would not have it. The tension and mistrust on both sides was evident throughout. The meeting did, however, allow those of its members who claimed to live in Pollok to decide for themselves whether or not to have their own branch. By a majority these 'Pollok' members decided to set up their own Branch. They then selected Joe Farrell as their candidate. The NOC had its way, but at a price.

The minute of the next NOC meeting — on March 27th — notes that Don Robertson in his report on the Glasgow meeting said that the members had decided additionally to set up branches in Hillhead, Cowcaddens, Glasgow South and Kelvingrove and to disband Glasgow.[19] No record of any such decision exists in Glasgow's minutes. The first the members heard of what they realised was the leadership's Balkanisation policy was a letter from Party Secretary Neil of March 31st saying that two Glasgow branches, South and Pollok, had been established.[20]

This maneouvering is interesting in a number of ways. Firstly, it indicates how the inner core of the leadership, in this case, Robertson (the Chairman), Neil (the Secretary), and Brown could take advantage of their membership of various committees in the party to make their own policy and then represent it to several parts of the party as the decision of other parts. Secondly, the policy of Balkanising Glasgow made it abundantly clear to many members — for example Richard Cotter, Gerry Finn and Jim Mackechnie who were to hold office in the Kelvin Branch, that they were distrusted and were being isolated — and that, in turn, made them suspicious of the leadership. Thirdly, it enabled the leadership to pick their own man to fight the Darnley by-election: that they should choose a

18. Interview with Don Robertson.
19. Minute of NOC Meeting of 27th March, 1976.
20. Neil, A. Letter of 31st March, 1976.

university lecturer to fight this depressed working class area speaks worlds about their limitations. Finally, the NOC's decision to abolish a branch without consulting it shows who was running the party.

But if the problems of the Glasgow Branch were to rebound against the leadership — as they were — this was in the future. For the first four months these problems were not much in evidence. The party, energetically led by Sillars and Neil, got on with Branch formation with some success. Precisely how many members joined is a matter of dispute. The precise number of members of any party is always a matter of dispute. Parties are inclined to treat membership numbers the way some people treat totem poles: the more you have the bigger a man you must be. The Labour Party has long indulged in exaggerations of its membership numbers: each Constituency Party affiliates to the party on the basis of its having *at least* one thousand members. Very few reach that number. Most have many fewer. Constituency Labour Parties (CLP's) in Scotland are particularly badly off. Only eight CLP's in Scotland — Berwick and East Lothian (2100: the largest), South Ayrshire (1800), Central Ayrshire, Kilmarnock, Kirkcaldy, Glasgow Cathcart, Edinburgh East and Larnark — had a membership of more than one thousand in 1976. A recent study has suggested that three-quarters of Scotland's CLP's have fewer than 400 members. It calculated that the average in Scottish CLP's is 489.[21]

The SNP also played the totem pole game with its membership into the late 1960's. For a while, the issuing of press statements with claims for vastly increased numbers provided a surrogate to by-election victories as a source of favourable publicity. Since the early 1970's, when it became clear that the totem pole game was not worth playing for the growth had to stop somewhere, and when it did the opposition made play with the lack of new growth, the SNP has stopped publishing its membership figures regularly. Instead, it makes a rough estimate of numbers — in late 1977 this estimate was "between 70,000 and 80,000". Whatever the short run temptation to parties to play the totem pole game, there are real problems in compiling an accurate list of members. Is a 'member' whose dues are in arrears, a member? Does a member who moves away lose his membership immediately, or only after he has joined a new branch? When does an inactive paid-up member cease to be counted as a member? For reasons such as this membership figures of all parties should always be treated with caution. In the case of the SLP, claims

21. Martin, C. and Martin, D., "Decline of Labour Party Membership" *The Political Quarterly,* Vol. 78, No. 4, October-December, 1977, pp. 459-471. See also, Ascherson, N., *Scotsman,* 20 September, 1977, p. 1.

were certainly exaggerated. By February 1st an SLP newsletter claimed that membership "should soon approach 2,000". Three months later, the claim was that "2,000 is a fair estimate". Only a month after that on June 9th the *Scotsman* reported a "membership they now claim to be in the region of 3,000". On August 19th the claims were smaller, but Ascherson wrote of ". . . a membership of 2,000 devoted followers."

As a matter of fact the actual membership of the party in June 1976 was less than a third of the "claim to be in the region of 3,000". It was 743. In that month the SLP office gave John Nairn a list of members by area. Nairn was then on the party's Finance Committee and he needed the list to help Alex Neil chase up branch secretaries in areas where the party was getting less than average contributions. This is the list Neil gave Nairn. Most of the 'areas' listed are parliamentary Constituencies; in some places however, most notably in Ayrshire, the membership is given by village.

Aberdeen	31	Glenrothes	7
Airdrie	4	Hamilton	4
Arbroath	1	Irvine/Kilwinning	8
Ayr	29	Kilmalcolm/Bridge of Weir	5
Auchinleck	3	Kilmarnock/Stewarton	16
Bearsden	7	Kirkcaldy	9
Bonnybridge	8	Leven	2
Catrine	2	Motherwell/Wishaw	12
Cumbernauld	27	Muirkirk	3
Cumnock	54	Ochiltree	50
Coylton	3	Patna	42
Drongan	5	Paisley	22
Dundee (Central)	30	Perth	5
Dundee (Whitfield)	25	Pollok	19
Dunfermline	3	South Ayrshire	21
Dunbarton (Central)	9	St. Andrews	20
Edinburgh (Central)	15	Stirling	4
Edinburgh (East)	2	Tillicoultry	10
Edinburgh (North)	19	West Lothian	6
Edinburgh (South)	20	Glasgow (Central)	1
Edinburgh (West)	4	Cathcart	6
Leith	9	Craigton	4
Pentlands	4	Govan	2
Edinburgh (Misc)	6	Garscadden	2
East Kilbride	22	Hillhead	17
Falkirk	4	Kelvingrove	18
Greenock	11	Maryhill	2

Glasgow (Misc)	12	Ross & Cromarty	4
Queen's Park	4	Berwick & E. Lothian	3
Springburn	1	Dumfries	2
Oban	2	Lanark	5
Midlothian	10	North Lanark	2
Inverness	1	Argyll	1
Moray	1	East Renfrew	4
England	10	West Renfrew	4
Galloway	3		

The most striking thing this membership list shows is that 241 of the party's 743 members came from Ayrshire — very nearly a third. Another list was drawn up, this time giving the membership of each branch, for the October Congress. The October list which is given in Appendix B, shows the party as having 883 members. It credits Ayrshire branches with 276 members. It also shows large concentrations in University branches and branches in areas where there are high concentrations of students and academics. The branches in Aberdeen, Aberdeen University, Edinburgh South, Edinburgh North-Central, Glasgow University, Kelvin, St. Andrews University, Stirling and Stirling University had a total of 249 votes in October. Thus 525 of the Party's 883 members came either from Ayrshire or from branches dominated by intellectuals. Less than half the members belonged to other branches — and not a few of them would have been intellectuals. This breakdown shows the party's strengths and its weaknesses starkly. The party had two different kinds of members who were in it for different reasons — roughly personal loyalty and ideological affinity — and who had different expectations of it. Keeping this kind of organisation together would have required organisational skills of a high order. Unfortunately, for the party, its leaders did not possess these skills: on the contrary the party was hardly gathered when it began to splinter.

Chapter V:

Enter the Trotskyists

Seen from the NOC's vantage point, the greatest error that they made was in not foreclosing the possibility of Trotskyist infiltration. When the SLP was formed there were numerous Trotskyist groups active in Scotland: the International Marxist Group (IMG) International Socialists (IS) —later to become the Socialist Workers Party (SWP) — and the Scottish Workers' Republican Party (SWRP) amongst them. Two of them, IMG and the SWRP, decided to go to the SLP's Inaugural Meeting.

This decision was announced to the Inaugural Meeting by the IMG. A statement by IMG made clear their support and pointed to the reason why IMG members would be joining :

> The essential task of this and future meetings of the SLP is to work out concrete proposals for the widest possible unity in action of the labour movement against mass unemployment, against the £6 norm, against the destruction of the welfare state and against attempts to settle in advance the powers of an Assembly.[1]

This, Stewart Maclennan (IMG), urged, could be achieved by the SLP only if it adopted the widest possible measure of internal democracy. These events were recorded in an article in *Red Weekly* (the British IMG paper) on January 22nd. IMG's statement gave the impression that it had whole-heartedly decided to join — this was wishful. This entry of the revolutionary left was noted in press reports of the Inaugural Conference.

It was not well received by Sillars and Neil or by the NOC. They

1. Printed in *Red Weekly*, 22nd January 1976 p. 5.

were particularly annoyed that Harry Ewing had received publicity for his demand that Sillars disassociate the SLP from the IMG. The Minute of the Meeting of 24th January makes clear their apprehension that Trotskyist membership was spoiling the SLP's public image. This point was to be reiterated with increasing urgency at NOC meetings up to the Stirling Conference. The NOC's decision on January 24th to prevent Trotskyists and Communists from joining the Party was — the minute records — issued to the Press.[2] From the outset then there was an irreconcilable tension between IMG's intention to use the SLP for revolutionary ends and the Leadership's determination to keep a good Press image for their party.

The Press is habitually and dependably anti-socialist and is particularly hard on revolutionary confessional parties — that is, parties whose members adhere to a specific programmatic ideology. They, in turn, normally expect to be opposed by the Press. The more revolutionary their programme, the greater their difficulty with the Press. This is known and understood — if not liked — on both sides. Sillars' achievement in breaking from the Labour party on a 'respectable' confession (devolution) enabled his party to escape such Press antipathy. This achievement was a source of great strength. To safeguard it they had to exclude IMG. The prohibition on other groups such as the SNP and Communist Party were purely nominal since members of these had not joined.

As time went on and the leadership found its cherished policies challenged by some branches, these challenges were blamed on Trotskyist infiltration. In fact the IMG became the scapegoat for disagreements which the Leaders mistook for disloyalty. Having been disloyal themselves, they saw disloyalty everywhere. And yet they can hardly be blamed for suspecting it from the IMG.

To understand the role of the IMG in the SLP, we need to look first at how the IMG is organised. IMG purports to be democratic. Certainly, none of its members is in a position to dominate. On the contrary, it has an elaborate formal decision making structure. The Scottish members are organised into branches which meet regularly. There is an elected Scottish Committee (SC) of members of branches which meets monthly. Occasionally a meeting of all Scottish comrades — known as the Scottish Aggregate — is called. Decisions of the SC and SA are binding on Scottish members, but major matters are referred to the National Committee.

The National Committee (NC) of forty-seven members meets

2. Minute of NOC 27th January 1976 p. 1.

73

quarterly to consider strategic and policy issues. In 1976 this Committee had seven Scottish members. To use their party pseudonyms, they were Comrades MacPherson (a full-time employee), Ure, Larkin, Rodgers, Ball, Eastwood and Hardie. Of these seven, six — including MacPherson — were in the SLP. The NC is guided, some in the IMG say too strongly, by a Political Committee (PC) of eighteen. During 1976, one of these was a Scot. The NC is responsible to the Annual Aggregate.

Within this formal constitutional structure there is an informal structure of "tendencies". The existence of these informal groupings of like minded comrades is encouraged as an integral part of the democratic ideology of the IMG. The various tendencies have changing membership. In theory they are expected to accept and implement the decisions taken within the formal structure on specific policies and strategies. These tendencies are also international. The majority British tendency is in agreement with the majority international tendency. It agrees with the minority American tendency and the dominant tendency in Western Europe. The tendencies are denominated by letter names — as Tendency 'A' 'B' and so on. I have been able to trace tendencies up to letter 'F' in 1976.

Eight IMG members joined the SLP at the Grosvenor Meeting (they were concentrated in the Leith, Glasgow and Aberdeen branches) and later they were joined by others. Thirty were SLP members at one time or another but there were rarely more than half that number active simultaneously. These IMG members had SLP meetings as well as IMG meetings to attend — usually IMG meetings before SLP meetings to prepare "lines". They had trade union meetings and again, preliminary IMG/TU meetings. All regularly attended *ad hoc* 'class struggle' meetings and demonstrations as well. While all this was going on the tendencies were preparing their positions. One recent ex-IMG member told me that a committed member could expect to attend an average of 7-8 meetings a week. During the academic term three meetings a day was the rule. In addition members are required to make a contribution to the group's finances. The amount of this contribution changes. Once nominal, it has been as high as 10% of each member's income. Members are also expected to move around the country from city to city as suits the needs of the party.

The intensity of members' committment to IMG cannot be doubted. But the corresponding claim of democracy is strongly disputed by various ex-members. They claim that the party's complicated structure and its pretence of democracy serve effectively to exclude all but the most intensely committed from any role in IMG policy making. One must always beware the anger and exaggeration of ex-members of secret conclaves but this particular charge rings true. IMG policy is to circulate all members with documents which any member or tendency cares to submit. These submissions can be lengthy. For example, the June 1976 meeting (NC) was faced with three documents on the SLP. The shortest of these ran to 2,000 words. Discussion and voting at meetings takes place on the basis of previously submitted documents — and on amendments to them which are also sometimes circulated. This effectively excludes all but the most dedicated and articulate comrades. More important, it discriminates against workers in favour of students and unemployed graduates. IMG's paid employees, who are usually graduates, have an obvious advantage in this process. These complicated procedures stymie quick and decisive action in the face of external events. On occasion IMG seems more anxious to tinker with its own machinery than to get involved in the world outside: a bureaucracy without a bureau.

But even if the IMG was bureaucratic its Scottish members did decide to join the SLP. This decision was later damned as 'empirical and eclectic': in other words it was not sufficiently argued out in advance.[3] The guiding thought in the minds of the majority which led the Scottish IMG into the SLP was 'economic'. They attached very little weight to the devolution debate in analysing the new SLP. They saw the party as Socialist first and welcomed its emergence at a time when they expected a Right-wing Social Democratic Labour Government to flounder. The 'Scottish' element in the SLP programme was a secondary feature in their papers. The majority of the Scottish IMG believed that the Labour Government elected in February 1974 would be forced, indeed, was already being forced, to attack the living standards of the working class. They believed that this Government could not keep its support intact in the face of rising inflation, very high unemployment and cuts in the public services. They expected that rebellion against this Government would break out, most probably first of all in the public service unions such as NALGO. They hoped to be able to widen the split thus created in the labour movement and to encourage and strengthen the more revolutionary, class-conscious side. When Sillars broke with the Labour party, the IMG saw him, as Comrade MacPherson put it to

3. Comrade MacPherson, *Balance Sheet and Perceptives*, November 1976.

me, as 'Wedgie Benn with guts', his party would provide a better vehicle than they had previously expected to have, to move "in the direction of consistently Marxist and revolutionary politics".[4] That this opportunity arose in Scotland, though not a central feature of the SLP as the IMG saw it, was not entirely unexpected. A break in the ranks of the Labour Party in Scotland was thought more likely because the prospect of oil-wealth had raised Scottish workers' expectations and made them less willing to accept cuts imposed by the Government. The IMG analysis also toyed — if somewhat nervously — with the idea that Scottish Nationalism might lead to a genuine national liberation movement — and not simply remain a petty bourgeois reaction. They could, therefore, just about support it.

The tactics used by IMG in supporting the SLP reflected their own internal divisions and the haste in which they decided to join. In part their move consisted of a classical "entry" — as it has often been practised by Trotskyist and Communist groups. In part it consisted of open support. The two are quite incompatible. "Entrism" is a secret process. In it a small group joins a larger party to use that larger party for its own ends. Sometimes this involves trying to use the machinery of the larger party to effect some end of which the smaller party is incapable. Sometimes it involves a hope of actually taking over whole branches — or even all — of a larger party which is thought to be weak. Sometimes entrism is practised in order to 'raid' the larger party for its more revolutionary members. To be effective all of these strategies must be secret and the identity of the entering members must be protected — lest they be thrown out.

Within the Trotskyist, or Fourth International (FI) convention, an elaborate body of thought exists on the role of revolutionary groups. In this tradition there are thought to be three kinds of revolutionary organisation, each of which is appropriate to different objective conditions. In unpropitious circumstances the FI forces will be tightly organised as a vanguard in a Group such as the International Marxist *Group:* in more hopeful circumstances they will be reorganised into a larger more public body known as a League such as the Scottish Socialist *League*, while in really favourable conditions they will be transformed into a party. These categories, though rarely used mechanically in the way this scheme may suggest, provide a useful insight into what Scottish IMG was doing in the SLP. They were not — not merely, at any rate — practising 'entrism' because the majority of them thought conditions were ripe for a more active role

4. Interview with MacPherson.

in Scottish political life. Their reading of Sillars' move out of the Labour Party encouraged them in these hopes. Was there not a hope that his new party would contain significant numbers of genuine revolutionaries who could be drawn out of the SLP and into a revolutionary organisation?

But some Scots IMG members thought this interpretation was wide of the mark. They continued to urge withdrawal. Thus Comrades Coltrane and Ure asserted in their document "Away from the SLP — Towards the Workers' Vanguard" (June 1976)

> The IMG's initial orientation to the SLP was carried out on a purely empirical basis, and as such was opportunist. With no discussion inside the Scottish membership, far less the organisation nationally, a number of members, including several leading comrades joined this organisation. There was, however, no clear analysis of what the SLP represented, what forces it contained or what the strategy of socialists inside it should be.[5]

Though the general arguments advanced by Comrades Coltrane and Ure were rejected by the NC, the last point here was eventually accepted by all in the party.

Comrade MacPherson, the Scottish IMG's full-time organiser, admitted as much in an article in November 1976 "Balance Sheet and Perspectives":

> The sheer novelty of the formation of the SLP together with the weakness of our cadre, produced a situation where our initial response to the SLP was empirical and eclectic.[6]

Their initial confusion had not really been sorted out until June. By then three positions or tendencies were discernible.

The main line was set out in a document: "Political Committee Resolution on our Attitude to the SLP, as amended" introduced by Comrade Ball on behalf of the Political Committee and carried by the June 1976 NC. The IMG has an elaborate four option voting system: For, Against, Abstention , and No Vote. The PC document was carried by 18 votes for; 8 against; 3 abstentions and 1 no vote. The document explained the emergence of the SLP in class-struggle terms. It was a combination of the acute economic crisis with a Right-wing Labour Government which led to Sillars' break, it

5. Coltrane, J. and Ure, C., *"Away From the SLP — Towards the Workers' Vanguard"*, Paragraph 5.
6. MacPherson, C. *Op. Cit* p. 1.

77

asserted. Thus:

> while not posing a threat to the political domination of the Labour
> Party over the masses, the objective basis exists therefore for an
> organisation to develop on a scale qualitatively larger than that of
> the revolutionary Left groups and to contain within it significant
> forces of the vanguard.[7]

But, the document argued, this opportunity could not be exploited
by the SLP as constituted because the party was divided between a
Social Democratic leadership and a 'centrist' base. In the Trotskyist
canon 'centrist' is a term of mild abuse. The Labour Party as a
whole is condemned as Social Democratic — it is on the Right. But
those of its members — in the *Tribune* group for instance — who take
a radical line are a bit different. The point about them which 'centrist'
denotes is that though revolutionary in words they are Right-wing in
action. Thus they are to be distinguished from the true Left.
However, the PC's document suggested that the SLP's 'centrist'
members might be detached from Sillars and turned into a
revolutionary force. There is much debate in Trotskyist groups about
the status of 'centrists'. Most seem to feel that the 'centre' is not a real
position, and therefore a 'centrist' is a person who is moving from
Left to Right or vice-versa. Many centrists are, therefore, potential
recruits.

The PC document emphasised that some people had joined the
SLP because of Sillars' rejection of Labour's economic policies. The
members thus attracted were willing, even anxious, to go much
further than their leaders in fermenting trouble for the Government.
Comrade MacPherson had speculated in his "Premliminary Balance
Sheet and Assessment" (February?):

> We can also expect the SLP to attract many of the elements making
> up the 'New' Labour Left in Scotland, around the Edinburgh petty
> bourgeois, the *Red Papers* etc. The weakness of the revolutionary
> Left has allowed a large molecular radicalisation in the public sector,
> (social workers, teachers etc.) to remain atomised and without
> direction, these forces we can expect the SLP to attract very quickly.[8]

These 'centrist' elements fitted ill they thought into Sillars' party.
The PC document expected the two to clash.

7. IMG *Political Committee Resolution on our Attitude to the SLP* (as amended)
   Para. 1.
8. MacPherson, C. *A Preliminary Balance Sheet and Assessment* (as amended) p.
   2.

F

What should IMG do about this? The PC document urged that IMG build the left wing of the SLP while taking care not to break up the party.[9] Any such break-up would be a defeat for the left and a victory for the Labour party and should therefore be avoided. This paragraph of the PC document was replaced by the June NC with a much stronger line on an amendment by Comrade Jones. Jones successfully argued that the Sillars' leadership was too strong to make a 'building the left wing' policy sensible. IMG, he urged, must recognise the inevitably of a conflict with Sillars. IMG should seek to define the difference between Sillars' right wing and their own position and thus hope to rally the centrist base to IMG when the split occurred. Specifically, they should prepare for a split after the October Conference by:

> a. not unleashing an immediate central generalised clash with Sillars but choosing *particular* definite and limited issues for a clash *e.g.* on the 'Jobs and Industry' document;
> b. establishing a journal to homogenise the left wing of the SLP;
> c. gaining places within the SLP organisation *e.g.* candidates in elections, branch secretaries, etc. Such an orientation clearly means urging forces to avoid exclusion and expulsion from the SLP.[10]

The difficulty of such a line (either the PC position or the Jones amendment) was that commitment to it would necessitate freeing IMG members from other work. Resources were very scarce. The SLP NOC's immediate exclusion of IMG members complicated IMG's problems because it meant that some IMG comrades in Scotland — those selling *Red Weekly* for example — could not join the SLP. It was also necessary to continue the "implantation" and "colonisation" of Scottish Trade Unions already begun. This could only be accomplished if the PC were to "allocate serious resources to Scotland, including at least four experienced Comrades to the area". This was agreed by the June NC.

The second strain in IMG thinking was represented by Comrades Coltrane and Ure. Their document to the June NC was based on a much less flattering appraisal of Sillars' actions and his party's revolutionary potential. They placed Sillars' break from the Labour Party in the context of the devolution debate; and they attributed the Labour Party's panic concessions over devolution to fears of a further collapse of the Labour vote.[11] As a senior member of the

9. *Political Committee Resolutions*, paragraphs 4 and 5.
10. *Jones amendment to PC Resolution as amended*, Para. 4 P.1.
11. Coltrane, C. and Ure, C. *Op Cit* Paragraph 1.

Kelvingrove Constituency Labour Party, Coltrane was in a good position to know what was happening in the Labour Party.

Coltrane and Ure poured scorn on their comrades' view that the creation of the SLP represented a serious breach in the Scottish Left:

> The split of Sillars and Robertson in the middle of (the devolution) debate represented an opportunistic attempt by this section of the bureaucracy to save themselves from the Nationalist threat. This split occurred solely at the level of bureaucracy. Sillars and Co. did not mount any systematic fight inside the LP, but simply packed their bags and left, only then informing the working class. They received very little support at the base of the LP, even inside their own CLPs. A sprinkling of locally prominent individuals joined them, but nowhere did the majority of even one ward do so.
>
> The SLP has since then attracted very little support inside the working class.[12]

For these reasons Coltrane and Ure urged that IMG keep its forces inside the Labour Party and the trade unions and not get involved in Sillars' sectarian party. In addition they urged IMG to remember that they originally entered the Labour Party because that party — for all the failure of its Leadership — was at least seen by the working class as the mass party of their class. This remained true. No energy should be wasted on the SLP.

Instead Coltrane and Ure urged a return of IMG members to the Labour Party ("the mass organisation of the WC"); a campaign in the IMG journal (*Red Weekly*) against the SLP; the establishment in Glasgow of a Scottish Centre (at a cost of £1,500) and a movement of Comrades into areas of Scotland, such as Dundee, where the IMG was weak.[13] Like the model bureaucracy it was, the NC refused to admit a mistake. It dismissed "Away from the SLP — Towards the Workers' Vanguard" by 1 vote for to 26 against, 2 abstentions and 2 no votes.[14]

The third IMG position was taken up by Comrades of Faction "A" — Eastwood and Hardie. It was fundamentally similar to the PC position save that it was less hopeful of the response which could be expected from the 'centrist base'. Instead it urged IMG to defend Sillars against attacks from the Labour Party of splitting the Labour movement. It too was rejected by the NC by a vote of 5-21-2-2.[15]

When the SLP's NOC determined to throw out its IMG members they blamed most of the party's trouble on the IMG and on what the

12. *Ibid.*
13. *Op Cit* paragraph 9.
14. Minute of (IMG) National Committee, June 26/27, P.3.
15. *ibid.*

leaders called the 'lunatic left'. This use of the term 'lunatic left' was, of course, a smear. Alex Neil in particular, liked to contrast the 'lunatic left' with 'mainstream socialists'. The IMG's reputation for extremism and trouble-making, their secret methods of operation and the intensity of their members' commitment made them an easy target for such scapegoat charges. And yet we have seen three things so far which make the charges look a bit wild. There were only thirty IMG members in the SLP. They were divided amongst themselves and had such a cumbersome decision procedure as to make concerted action difficult. Finally, their imprecise plans were hard to execute. None of this was known to the leaders of the SLP.

They had another left wing cadre to contend with, though this was a less considerable one. The SLP was joined, *en masse*, at the Inaugural Meeting by the Scottish Workers' Republican Party (SWRP). The very name of the party invokes the traditions and associations of the Clydeside rebel, John Maclean. Maclean, born in Pollokshaws in 1879, is a much venerated patron saint of Scottish Socialism. Maclean rose from poverty to a post as a teacher with the Govan School Board. This job, and his freedom, he soon lost in the cause of his beliefs. He became the principal speaker in Scotland for the Social Democratic Federation for he could fill large halls with working men whom he would electrify with his teachings. As a Socialist, Maclean was opposed to the First World War. Unlike his fellow Scottish Socialist, Ramsay MacDonald, who also opposed the war and also spoke against it in Glasgow during the war, Maclean pushed his opposition until the police arrested him for sedition. Maclean's present status as a Socialist patron saint owes much to these persecutions and to the fact that Lenin appointed him Bolshevik Consul for Scotland in 1918. His reputation in his native land is higher still because, despite Lenin's accolade, he refused to join the *British* Communist Party on its foundation in 1920 — forming his own Scottish Workers' Republican Party instead. After his health was broken in prison, he died of a cold caught when campaigning as that party's candidate in the 1923 General Election.

Maclean exerted a powerful influence over the new SWRP and many in the SLP. So many of them, like Maclean, had sprung from poor working-class Clydeside backgrounds to be intellectuals; a school teacher in Maclean's case, teachers, students and journalists in theirs. This rise, which might have aroused so much suspicion in Socialist circles, had been legitimated by Maclean. Moreover, Maclean as an early Clydeside Socialist, had remained untainted —

as Ramsay MacDonald, certainly had not — by the later betrayal of that revolutionary tradition by the Labour Party. Maclean's freedom from the taint of the compromises of the Labour Party (and, for that matter, of the failures of the Communist Party) made him an ideal talisman for the new SWRP.

The new SWRP was a group of never more than twelve people which was formed in February 1974.[16] Its members were an ill-assorted combination of ex-IMG members and militant nationalists. At its first meeting the 'party' called itself the Scottish Socialist League; it changed the name at the second meeting. The SWRP was a propagandising organisation. Its members believed and believe that an independent Scotland is inevitable and work to make that as yet unborn country Socialist. They propagate their beliefs in a monthly journal, *Scottish Worker*, which first appeared in November 1974.

The SWRP had three candidates in the May 1974 local elections. M. Montgomery won 140 votes or 2.6% of the vote in the Kelvin/Woodside ward of Strathclyde Region. D. Anderson stood in the Woodside ward of Glasgow District and won 95 votes or 3.7% of the total. It was a matter of some pride that these candidates did better than the Communist Party candidates. In the regional contest, the Communist candidate, P. Noon, won 1.9% of the vote while in the district contest his comrade, L. Bain, took 1.7%. The SWRP also put up D. Leadbetter in the Central Region seat of Bridge of Allan/Logie. He came last in a four-cornered contest which the Conservative candidate won. Leadbetter took 51 votes — 1.9% of the total.[17] At the time the party's members were equally divided between Glasgow and Stirling; each had four! The May election exhausted the party's funds, though the leafleting resulted in a number of new members joining the party. Without money for the deposit the party could not nominate candidates for the October 1974 General Election. It leafleted urging voters to abstain.

In September 1974 the party split. The immediate cause of the split was a disagreement over tactics at the September 7th Hyde Park Anti-Fascist demonstration. The party line was to avoid violence. Two members of the demo couldn't accept this. As these two were the 'tartan' members of the party, they were odd partners for the ex-IMG members. The Hyde Park argument served to crystallise the political

16. This account of the SWRP is based mainly on interviews with Charlie Gordon, Norman Easton and Jim McKechnie and also on *Scottish Worker*, Dec. 1975-Oct. 76.
17. Bochel, J. and Denver, D. *Scottish Local Government Elections 1974* (Edinburgh 1975), pages 24, 30, 104.

division. The 'tartans' were thrown out. It was a victory for the socialist element of the SWRP over its nationalist contingent.

It was after this split that *Scottish Worker* was started. Jim Mackechnie (later to be Chairman of the Kelvin Branch of the SLP) was to be its editor. Other important contributors were Charlie Gordon, Alan Morrison and Norman Easton. All also wrote under pseudonyms to make the paper look more considerable. In addition, Easton outlined the party's policy in a 23-page cyclostyled pamphlet, *Socialism, Nationalism, Scotland and Independence*. After Charlie Gordon joined toward the end of 1974 the party began to move toward the FI International Minority tendency — of which Gordon had been an adherent in his IMG days. Under this influence the party applied for membership of the Scottish section of the Fourth International. This move cost the party about half its membership, including Jim Mackechnie. It was down to five. In May 1975 Alan Morrison stood as the SWRP candidate in a local government by-election in Grangemouth and won a mere 9 votes.

After discussion between December 1975 and the SLP's Inaugural Conference, the SWRP decided to go to the Inaugural Meeting. As we have noted, no one was allowed into the Inaugural Meeting unless he joined the party and paid £2. The SWRP members paid up and its remaining members joined the SLP. They were uneasy about what they saw as Sillars' social democracy but submerged that ill ease because they believed his party to be fundamentally at one with theirs. At two meetings, one on January 31st and the other on February 3rd, they decided to 'enter' the SLP. This decision meant that they would cease to meet as a separate organisation; but, of course, they continued to produce their journal *Scottish Worker*. There is a disagreement between the SWRP members I talked to about just what was decided.[18] Charlie Gordon and Norman Easton both of whom are still very prominent within the SLP, deny that there was an intention to 'enter' the SLP in the Trotskyist sense of 'enter'. Ed Robertson and Matt Montgomery, who were also present when the decision was taken, insist that the original idea was to 'enter' as an organised group with the conscious intention of splitting off after a while with some additional members gained while in the SLP. Gordon, Easton and Morrison do not deny, however, that one of their motivations in joining the SLP was to help kick the IMG out of it. Montgomery argued against the 'entry' on the grounds that the

18. Interviews with Charlie Gordon, Norman Easton, Ed Robertson and Matt Montgomery.

83

SWRP was too small to execute the procedure successfully, especially while the SLP were so young and unformed. Though he was, at the time, the SWRP's organiser and had been one of its two founding members, he was so angry at the decision of his party to 'enter' the SLP that he resigned from the SWRP and joined IMG. Ed Robertson stayed in the SWRP and he insists that the party met at least twice after it 'entered' the SLP to concert its activities in the SLP.

Whether or not the members of the SWRP met as such, they did continue to produce *Scottish Worker* and their meeting to produce the paper provided more than enough cover for them to concert their line on the SLP. Before long the masthead of the paper was changed from "paper of the Scottish Workers' Republican Party" to "for a Socialist Scotland". In March 1976 it urged "Build the Scottish Labour Party". The SWRP's former members have been welcomed into the SLP. Charlie Gordon was an SLP candidate in the May 1977 local elections and secretary of the Glasgow West Branch. Alan Morrison became a member of the SLP's Standing Orders Committee. He also became Chairman of the vote tellers at the SLP's first Congress and won the highest number of votes for the National Executive Committee (the body elected to replace the NOC). Norman Easton was elected to the NEC in October 1977.

II

The battle between the divergent parts of the SLP did not take long to develop. The first battleground was the Darnley by-election. It was held on June 1st for a vacancy on Glasgow District Council caused by the conviction of the sitting Councillor Baillie Kane on corruption charges. At the previous election the seat had been carried safely by Labour. There were 10,000 electors, and as Alec Neil informed the Special NOC meeting of March 13th the result in the previous vote had been:

Labour	3,159
SNP	1,323
Conservative	456
Communist	56

It was thus an ideal seat for the new party to fight. The Labour Party was generally discredited and the SLP may have thought that voters in this badly treated council housing area would be feeling betrayed by their ex-councillor. Moreover, a SLP intervention was hardly likely, of itself, to throw the seat to the SNP, as Labour's previous vote had been more than twice that of the Nationalists.

The decision to fight Darnley was not taken without opposition. Matt McLure objected that the party should reserve its strength for a forthcoming General Election. His reservations were not shared by other members of the NOC, despite the fact that Sillars had warned them earlier in the meeting that:

> Momentum was building up in Westminster for a General Election possibly in April but most probably in the autumn.[19]

Most members shared Sillars' and Neil's belief that the party needed to "prove its electoral credibility" before it faced a General Election. The reiterated belief that a General Election was imminent was an important factor in the SLP's early history. It helps to account for the generally slipshod and hurried way a number of important decisions were taken. This belief added to the hurry already built into the party by its leaders' apprehension that the Nationalists had nearly completed their scoop of previously Labour working-class voters.

This appreciation was not shared by the SNP. Indeed a number of their leaders feared that the SLP had been successful enough in the timing and manner of its launch to cut off any possible movement of working-class voters out of the Labour Party and into the SNP. These fears gave the SLP's leaders a fair amount of leverage with these SNP leaders. Was a pact advisable? Would the SNP stand down in certain seats crucial to the SLP, while the SLP for its part concentrated its fire on Labour seats which the SNP couldn't expect to win? Could such an understanding provide a bridge into the SNP in case the SLP floundered? Or into the SLP for the SNP's Social Democrats if the SNP turned rightward? Did Sillars really suggest dual-membership in the SLP and SNP when he addressed a "members only" meeting of the Andrew Fletcher Society on October 22nd 1976? Does this perceived common interest explain why the SLP's leaders did not back their Cumbernauld branch's attempt to embarrass the SNP-controlled District Council? Does it make sense of the SLP's decision, shortly thereafter announced, to stand only in Labour seats where the SNP was not a stronger challenge? All this is

19. Minute of NOC of 13th March 1976.

speculative, of course, but these were speculations and suspicions which many of the SLP's subsequently disaffected members held.

Naturally, political speculation focused on suspected deals between the SLP and the SNP leaders. But this focus only shows the extent to which we have yet to digest the implications of the passing of two-party politics.[20] In a two-party system there is normally no need for one party to negotiate with the other. They are enemies. When one is in power the other is out — and that is about all there is to it. Certainly, as long as two-party competition prevails any hint of a pact between the leaders of the parties smacks of betrayal, and is rightly resented by the members of both parties. But when many parties compete, things become much more complicated. Typically, in a multi-party system each party represents a specific part of the electorate, but none can obtain a majority of seats in the legislature — or votes — on its own. In such a world, deals between the party leaders are not only normal but inevitable if any kind of majority administration is to be formed. In this case, the identity of interest and policy between the SNP and the SLP was so manifest that it would have been foolish not to seek to establish points of common interest. The problem for both, of course, was that no one had explained the necessity to the party workers — or voters.

But equally interesting as far as the SLP is concerned was its failure to back its Cumbernauld Branch's attempt to help their local dustmen, who were on strike. This was a decision which closed a door on one of the paths which the SLP might have followed. It is important, here, to note that the strike occurred right in the heart of the new Scotland — in the town in which, above all others, the SNP was entrenched. In 1976, Cumbernauld District was the only District in Scotland in which the SNP had a secure majority. The local National Party had built up a strong machine around Provost Gordon Murray and held on to the gains made in the late 1960s. Cumbernauld is ideal territory for the National Party and had proved impervious to the Labour Party's attempts to win it back. If the SLP had established itself here it would at once have raised its bargaining power vis-a-vis the SNP, shamed the Labour Party deeply, and shown that it could be a force in areas of Scotland very different from its Ayrshire base.

The chance to make this point came just as the SLP was girding itself to fight the Darnley by-election. The SNP-controlled

20. For an admirably lucid and concise discussion of these implications see Pulzer, P. *Political Representation and Elections in Britain*, London 1972. pages 56-61.

Cumbernauld Council proposed to cut the wages of their dustmen, claiming that the Labour government's public expenditure cuts left them with no choice. The dustment went out on strike. The issues were complicated for the SLP because the local official of the union concerned (GMWU) urged the strikers to accept the Council's offer for fear of greater cuts if they refused. Nonetheless, without consulting the NOC, the thirty-strong Cumbernauld SLP branch decided to back the strikers.[21] Could the party afford not to grasp this opportunity to distinguish itself from the SNP? Could it afford to pass up the chance to demonstrate that it was opposed to the government's expenditure cuts? Should it not grasp the opportunity to build up the credibility of its Cumbernauld branch and demonstrate to Socialists all over Scotland that here indeed was a party which had broken out of the rigid pattern of the Labour Party? But, as well as these arguments in favour of supporting the strike, there were important arguments against it. Could the party risk any of its scarce manpower when it was committed to fighting a by-election campaign at Darnley? Could it risk any chance of a pact with the SNP? Given the NOC's fears about Trotskyist infiltration, could it dare support militant action which might serve to draw more Trotskyists into the party? (One of the ways the IMG were trying to attract the SLP's 'centrist' elements away from Sillars was by reminding him at public meetings of his failure to support the Glaswegian firemen in their strike several years before. The IMG line is to support all strikes.) Also, was it not dangerous for the whole delicate fabric of the new party's organisation to let a branch present the central organisation with a *fait accompli?*

In this important test of the party's will it opted for the safe conventional course of action. The party did not support its branch's action: the strike collapsed. Instead, the party threw all its energy into the Darnley by-election.

This commitment also helps partly to explain why the SLP did not take a stronger position in support of sit-ins in Colleges of Education. On the 13th of May, students of Moray House College of Education in Edinburgh had begun a sit-in to protest at the effects of the government's public expenditure cuts. These cuts meant that education authorities in Scotland were hiring few teachers that spring for the following autumn. Indeed, the news which ensured support for the Moray House students' action, was the

21. Nairn, T. "Binmen Fight Wage Cuts", Scottish Worker, June 1976 Page 3 and Nairn, J. "Cumbernauld: Union Bureaucracy Sell Out Strike", Scottish Worker, July 1976 Page 7.

announcement by Strathclyde region the morning the sit-in began that it would be hiring no new primary teachers that year. The sit-in at Moray House quickly spread to other Colleges of Education in Scotland and then to England. A sit-in by this normally politically inert group of students was a most unusual and important development. Alerted immediately to what was happening by Scott Brady and David Ross of his Moray House 'SLP society' Sillars sent a much appreciated telegram of support. His was the first encouragement from a well-known figure which the students received. Here again was an opportunity for the SLP to use a campaign to identify itself with an important group in Scotland (students and teachers) and to embarrass the Labour government. In this case the SLP actually had the initiative but it failed to follow through. The initiative passed to Margaret Bain (SNP MP for Dunbartonshire East) and Robin Cook (Labour MP for Edinburgh Central). Again, the Darnley by-election campaign which occurred at the same time, may be an important reason.

Perhaps another reason why the party's leaders were unwilling to get drawn into either the Cumbernauld dustmen's strike, or the Moray House students' sit-in, was that they were again having difficulties with their north Glasgow members. The remainder of the branch, after Pollok had been hived off, protested about this hiving off to the NOC. They particularly resisted the NOC's proposal for further division of the Glasgow membership. For its part, the leadership, and particularly Alex Neil, came increasingly to refer to members of this branch as part of the 'lunatic left'. Comrade MacPherson's description of it as the 'atomised left' was more to the point. They did not co-ordinate their activities. When a four-man delegation from the branch was heard by the NOC on April 24th, Sillars told the NOC before the delegates were let into the room that three of the delegates were not to be trusted, they were Trotskyites. The fourth, Charlie Gordon, was OK. The three others actually represented the views of most members of the branch. The minute of this NOC meeting notes that "each spoke in favour of their respective points of view".[22] However, only Gordon's individual views were recorded. "C. Gordon argued that it was better to have a branch for those parts of the city where there were sufficient members to form one and that erring on the side of anarchy would be more fruitful at this stage of development."[23] The protests were rejected along with a

22. *Minute of NOC Meeting, 24th April 1976, P.1.*
23. *Ibid.*

88

compromise plan offered by Joe Farrell (Glasgow Branch Chairman and Darnley candidate who was a member of the NOC). Accepting their defeat the dissidents constituted themselves as a Kelvin branch on Friday, May 14th. They then immediately wrote to the NOC demanding that the NOC recognise the right of each branch to have observers at the NOC meetings. Their disaffection deepened during the Darnley election struggle but it was not strong enough to prevent many branch members from working in the campaign.

They were not alone. SLP members came from all over Scotland to work for the new party in its first fight. A bus load of workers came from as far as Aberdeen. One of the party's most unlikely recruits, Litster Gardiner, also worked regularly in Darnley. Gardiner was quickly to gain prominence in the party as Secretary of the Stirling Conference's Standing Orders Committee (SOC). Born and educated in Edinburgh, his frequent appearances in Darnley were made at the cost of some personal inconvenience. It was a long drive from Blindcrake in Allerdale District, Cumbria. Gardiner is the senior partner of a large Keswick legal firm. He was also at the time Secretary of the Independent group on the Allerdale District Council. The new party seems to have reawakened his Scottish Socialism. He and many others worked hard for the SLP's 14% of the vote at Darnley. Outwardly it was quite a creditable performance for a party at its first outing. Underneath the pressure was beginning. Gardiner's opinion is categorical: "The trouble began at Darnley."

III

The troubles which plagued the SLP crystallised over its policy discussion document: "Jobs and Industry".[24] In preparation for a policy discussion conference to be held in Middleton Hall, Gorebridge, Midlothian, on the weekend of May 15th-16th, the NOC approved "Jobs and Industry" at its April 27th meeting. The paper was written by Neil with help from Sillars. Unlike a number of other of the SLP policy papers which bear the mark of work Neil had done before leaving the Labour Party, "Jobs and Industry" was original to the SLP.

It contained the fullest expression of the Party's industrial and

24. The Scottish Labour Party, "Jobs and Industry: A Policy for Full Employment" (April 1976).

economic ideas. It was the SLP's Socialism. Its purpose, announced in its introduction, was "to eliminate the age-old Scottish fear of unemployment". But some jobs were more important to the party's leaders than others:

> In five years 71,000 jobs were lost in manufacturing, which contributed to the total of 106,000 plus lost in the productive sector of the Scottish economy. Job losses here were partly offset by a gain of 77,000 in service industries such as banking, insurance, public administration and professional services. The net loss of jobs in the Scottish economy over this period was 36,000. We have a net job loss and a weakened industrial base.[25]

Good solid jobs in manufacturing industry were better than service industry jobs. The party's ideology was of a piece. It sought to create jobs for the kind of people it hoped would join the party. "Jobs and Industry" was about running the Scottish economy within the context of a devolution settlement. It proposed the establishment of no fewer than ten new agencies of government. Some, like a much strengthened SDA, would be run by appointed boards; others were to be subject to close political scrutiny. The SDA was to be "the main instrument of regeneration in the Scottish economy".

Much more controversial within the SLP were the document's polite bows in the directions both of the "Small and Medium-sized Business Sector" and of "Multi-National Corporations". The former were to be protected and nourished. The latter (echo of "Don't Butcher . . .") were welcomed into Scotland — though they were to be urged to accept more worker participation. Protecting small business was a new line for a Socialist document in Brtiain, though it was one the Government was gingerly toying with at the same time. Encouraging multi-nationals was, however, anathema to almost every Socialist. Introducing the idea here was bound to cause trouble. Even more trouble arose around "Jobs and Industry's" line on control of financial institutions. Feebly it stated:

> The SLP will press for the Scottish Parliament to have the power to take financial institutions into public ownership. But as the present Labour Government has no intention of such a challenge to capitalism in the British context, it is highly unlikely that the Scottish Government Act will give us powers they have never dared to reach for.[26]

Though the document went on to urge the purchase of one major banking group, the main problem was clear; the document was so

25. *Op cit* p.5.
26. *Op cit* p.21.

mild on both its Socialist and Nationalist fronts that, if adopted, it would leave the SLP open to being outmanoeuvred by both the Labour and National Parties.[27] Unluckily, for the leaders this happened even before the October Conference. The Labour Party's Annual Conference in September voted to nationalise the banks, and the National Party repeatedly stressed the greater flexibility of an independent Scottish government.

Tom Nairn, a member of the Edinburgh South branch and a much respected political theorist, gently chided his leaders in a critique of "Jobs and Industry" when he pointed out that lacking any well-developed system of internal communications, the party leaders were forced to speak to their members through the press and this meant that they had to say the sort of 'moderate' and 'sensible' things the press would approve of: hence the feebleness of "Jobs and Industry".[28] It is only fair to add that men who have been engaged in months of frenetic activity putting together a party, cannot be expected to write well-researched, careful documents. Nevertheless they produced it, and having produced it, they defended it.

IV

The long-planned policy conference, the first meeting of the local activists except in their own branches, was held at Middleton Hall on the weekend of May 15th and 16th. The reconstituted Kelvin branch met for the first time the previous (Friday) evening. At its first meeting the Kelvin delegates agreed, with some misgivings, to the distribution at Middleton Hall of a document which had been written by Sean Tierney called "Who Runs Glasgow?".[29] Although unhappy about its wording, they endorsed its thesis. This document was an attempt to make delegates from the other branches aware of what was happening in north Glasgow. "Who Runs Glasgow?" was unsigned and distributed by Kelvin delgates Jim Mackechnie and Richard Cotter after lunch on Sunday. But since it was not

27. An admirable critique, on which this account is largely based, was written by Tom Nairn *"Comments on the SLP: Jobs and Industry Draft Policy Statement"*. It was never presented to the NOC.
28. *Op cit* pp. 7, 8.
29. *"Who Runs Glasgow?" (A statement by some SLP members in Glasgow)* (Sean Tierney).

distributed till then it did not mar the whole meeting.

The conference opened by agreeing to an emergency resolution supporting students at Moray House and Dundee Colleges of Education in the occupation of their colleges.[30] It also heard from Sillars that the Scottish Council of the Labour Party's decision to back a strong measure of devolution at their March Conference was a step in the right direction.

One subject at the Conference was money. Secretary Alex Neil emphasised the need both to raise money and to spend it sensibly. Local full-time agents were an extravagance. Only (sic) three officers other than secretarial staff were needed.[31] Of all the statements made by Neil on behalf of the SLP — that they had 3,000 members, for example — this was easily the most extraordinary. The truth, as he had informed the April NOC, was that the party had a bank balance of £897. It also had an outstanding bill for £310. Since the party had a balance of £550 on January 24th it is evident that the money-raising activities of the party were just about keeping up with expenses even though there was only one full-time employee (Neil).

Neil did reveal to the Middleton delegates that there were still places available in the party's '300' club. The idea of the '300' club was that each of 300 members would contribute £1 each month; at the end of each month a prize, or several prizes, would be drawn on the money raised.[32] Since the value of the prizes was fixed, the empty places were costing the party money. It is not surprising therefore that the '300' club became a '200' club at the July 17th NOC meeting — and still there were vacant places. This was a clear case where Neil's lack of frankness with the NOC was hurting the party. The idea behind century clubs is that an organisation which creates one can

30. The Emergency Motion (which was not printed in the minutes of the Middleton Hall meeting) read:
    The delegates at this first conference of the Scottish Labour Party (fully) support the action of the students of Moray House and Dundee Colleges of Education in their efforts not only to secure employment for teachers in training, but also to reverse the vicious attack by the Labour Government on Education and the Social Services.
    To this end the SLP members of Parliament will pursue their opposition to the public expenditure cuts at Westminster and Branches will be asked to send moral and/or material support.

    Proposed — David Ross
    Seconded—Scott Brady

    (Branches were not asked to send moral and/or material support.)
31. *SLP Report on the Conference held in Middleton Hall, 15th and 16th May 1976,* pp.2-3.
32. Cyclostyled to SLP members "300 Club — Information" by Alex Neil. p.2.

expect about 10% of its members to join. Thus '300' would have been the right venture for the SLP only if Neil's claim of 3,000 members had been justified. As we have seen, the party had 743 members and therefore had no business having a century club at all.

Money was a real problem for the SLP. The full extent of the problem was carefully disguised from the NOC. The July NOC was blandly told there was no need for panic measures — it then agreed to allow Jim Sillars to pay half the office rent. In fact the party's finances seem to have reached their nadir that month. Neil told Don Robertson early in July, that the Party had no money and that it would have to be wound up. Robertson's somewhat surgical suggestion that the situation might be retrieved if Neil became a part-time employee, and the office vacated, was not accepted.[33] Instead the party weathered this problem by gaining loans from Robertson himself and from Litster Gardiner. It also begged its middle-class intellectual members to increase the amount of their Standing Orders to the party.

The SLP's money problem threw a large shadow over the whole enterprise. Almost all of the senior members of the party had had their most recent political experience in the Labour Party. That party supports itself — badly as "James Alexander" showed — largely by money given to it by the trades unions. The money it raises from individual members is usually derisory. South Ayrshire CLP is an exception to this — its large annual turnover could have transformed the SLP's financial position. But the SLP deliberately turned its back on trade union membership and the South Ayrshire CLP. In its stead it hoped for support from the Standing Orders of — a dozen — friends. This was hopeless. Why the Middleton delegates had to be so misled on the subject remains a mystery.

Saturday afternoon at the Middleton Conference was given over to watching a televised Scotland v England football match. At least the SLP had learned some of the lessons of the Labour Party's devolution debate! Later the Conference divided into four groups to discuss different parts of "Jobs and Industry". Three of the four groups reported against the section of the document they had been asked to consider. The conclusions of these discussions were passed on to Don Robertson for circulation to party members. They were never circulated.

The meeting also discussed electoral strategy, and thereby revealed more contradictions. Jim Sillars, in his Parliamentary Report, had

33. Interview with Don Robertson.

93

observed:

> There is a strong possibility of a General Election in October/November and during the next few months we must show a high Scottish and high Socialist profile. It is doubtful if the Labour Government will be able to put through (the) Devolution Bill. . . .[34]

But, during the strategy discussion, the Conference agreed:

> At (the) time of (the) Assembly, Scotland will be a multi-party state. (The) SLP is not Westminster orientated — our main aim must be power in (the) Assembly.[35]

But, if the government couldn't deliver devolution, was not the talk of the SLP as a mass party with seats in the Edinburgh Assembly just a little premature?

The final session of the Conference, on the Sunday afternoon, was to be a trailer for the Stirling Annual Conference. The mood of the final session was set during the last interchange before lunch. Richard Cotter, on behalf of Kelvin Branch, had asked the Conference to approve one of the proposals which the delegates from Glasgow had put to the NOC — that NOC meetings be open to members of the party. He claimed that this would allay suspicions. Sillars would have none of it. He told the Conference that they had had nothing but trouble from Glasgow from the beginning. "If we had open NOC meetings," he went on, "I for one would remain mum because I know every word would be reported in the next week's "Red Weekly" [36] The Conference backed its leader. But after this outburst, Cotter and Jim Mackechnie felt justified in distributing their document "Who Runs Glasgow?". They distributed their copies to delegates they hoped would be sympathetic and to others who asked for it.

The tone of the document can be judged from its concluding sentences:

> This leaves the General Secretary with some egg on his face, but more important is the fact that an attempt had been made to prevent the largest group of members in Glasgow from being represented at an important Party discussion. We do not think that this manoeuvre is attributable to bloody-mindedness, but regard it as a deliberate attempt to smother the demands of the Glasgow members.[37]

"Who Runs Glasgow?" spoiled a real case by overstating it. Don Robertson, then in the Chair, saw the document and asked delegates

34. SLP *"Report of the Conference"* p.1.
35. *Op cit* p.7.
36. Interview with Ian Miller and Don Robertson.
37. "Who Runs Glasgow?".

G

— some of whom hadn't seen it — to ignore it. It was out of order and unsigned. The fact that not all delegates had been given a copy made it easier for the Chair to dismiss the document. Sillars and Neil were not so cool. After conferring they attacked the Glasgow delegates' position: "The SLP was historically and politically necessary." Sillars threatened that unless the documents were condemned he would resign from the party. Thus placed on the agenda, "Who Runs Glasgow?" was condemned by the delegates for its vicious attacks on Alex Neil. More than a few delegates left the Conference aghast that a very rewarding weekend had been so angrily interrupted.

V

One final piece of the SLP puzzle must be put into place before we look at the crisis at the October Stirling Conference. This is what became Resolution No. 41 on the Agenda of that Conference: Kelvin branch's critique of "Jobs and Industry". Resolution No. 41 was agreed by Kelvin branch at their August 22nd meeting.

Each branch was allowed to submit two resolutions to Conference. Branches who wished to submit more were politely reminded by Alex Neil of the limitations of time in a two-and-a-half-day Conference. With this limitation in mind the Kelvin delegates had to choose between seven resolutions which members had submitted. All were agreed in principle; their job was to place the seven in some kind of order. This was made easier by "Compositing" several of the proposals.

Resolution No. 41 was a Composite of a proposal of Branch Chairman Jim Mackechnie with a proposal of Alan Freeman. Freeman's right to remain a member of the SLP had been challenged by the NOC. Alex Neil wrote to him on March 27th asking him "to clarify the situation". Was he a member of IMG? Freeman did not deny past membership of IMG; he did not deny close association with its members nor agreement with their views. He asserted his "wish to maintain an association with the IMG as far as is compatible with membership of the SLP". On this basis he had "left the IMG when it became clear that the organising committee — very wrongly in my opinion — would not accept members of the IMG within the SLP".[38] When this was explained to Neil he accepted Freeman's

38. Open letter by Alan Freeman to the Kelvin Branch, p.1.

assurance — what else could he do? — and allowed him to be reinstated. The decision was reported to the July NOC.

The business of formally holding a membership card in the party played many roles in the SLP. There were not a few prominent people, journalists mainly, who have told me they were sympathetic enough to the SLP to have Standing Orders for several pounds a month to the party, but who were not formally card-carrying members of the party because being so would have embarrassed them professionally. On the other hand, there were people, like Freeman, who as members of the SLP claimed to have left the IMG. Whether their leaving of IMG, was any more real than the journalists not being card-carrying members of the SLP, is a nice question. Certainly the non-IMG members of the Kelvin branch were never sure whether the "ex-IMGers" in their ranks still were acting as IMG entrists into the party.

The proposals of Mackechnie and Freeman differed more in emphasis and style than substance. Mackechnie's was like a good many left-wing resolutions sent every year to the Labour Party's Annual Conference. It called for the SLP Conference to affirm:

> . . . its belief that only thorough-going Socialist policies, fundamentally based on the common ownership of the means of production, distribution and exchange, can offer a sure and sound foundation for the development of a planned economy. . . .[39]

and asked that this belief lead to:

(1)   the nationalisation of private industries, land, the banks and financial institutions . . .
(2)   government control of investment . . .
(3)   . . . direction of industry to areas of multiple deprivation
(4)   an expansion of social services . . .
(5)   withdrawal from the EEC and establishment of bi-lateral trade contracts with countries with non-capitalistic economic systems.

Freeman's proposal called for:

> . . .fighting socialist policies and united action to defeat these vicious attacks on living standards and conditions.[40]

and more precisely asked the SLP to:

> Pledge itself to work for, and participate in, the broadest possible

---

39. Proposed Congress Resolution submitted to the Kelvin Branch of the SLP by Jim McKechnie.
40. Proposal by Alan Freeman.

unity of the Labour movement in support of these aims.

As a basis for a united fightback against the attacks of the Labour Government it urges support for and resolves to campaign for the adoption by the Labour movement of resolution 17 of the STUC Perth conference. . . .[42]

Support for Resolution No. 17 of the STUC Congress had become the touchstone of Scottish IMG's policy.

These two positions were stitched together. Slightly modified they appeared as Resolution No. 41. The full text of STUC Resolution No. 17 also became SLP Resolution No. 43. It was moved by Aberdeen. STUC No. 17 called for (a) the 35-hour week, (b) longer holidays, (c) no redundancies, (d) an opening of the books of any company declaring redundancies, (e) nationalisation without compensation of companies who paid poor wages, (f) restoration of the cuts in public expenditure, (g) ending incomes policy limits on wage rises, (h) full cost of living cover for all state benefits.[43] It was at least as left-wing as Kelvin's Resolution. And neither resolution was any more 'extreme left-wing' than Stirling's Resolution No. 39, which called for wholesale nationalisation of banking, insurance, the petro-chemical, electronics and automobile industries "among the first acts of a Scottish Socialist Government", and Cumnock's Resolution No. 45, which was on similar lines.[44]

Thus the fact that the struggle within the SLP centred on Kelvin is an indication of the very considerable extent to which the party's problems had become political — rather than principled. The question became not just "Who Runs Glasgow?" but "Who Runs the SLP?".

42. *Ibid.*
43. Resolutions for SLP Congress No. 43.
44. Resolutions for SLP Congress Nos. 39 and 45.

Chapter VI:

The Crisis: Death by the Splinter

On September 20th, Jim Sillars, Alex Neil and David McKay — the SLP's candidate in a local government by-election in Irvine — held a press conference in Glasgow. The conference was used to boost McKay's candidature for the by-election which was to be held the next day and to introduce the resolutions which had been tabled for the forthcoming Annual Congress in Stirling.[1] In the event McKay came last with 1,112 votes behind McLeod (SNP) 3,854, McKie (Labour) 2,935 and Loach (Cons) 2,531. At another by-election in Clydebank, held on the same day, the SLP candidate, Conroy, came fourth out of five candidates with 71 votes. The Nationalist candidate, Butcher, won with 299 votes to Burke (Labour) 277, Simpson (Cons) 178 and Crawford (Comm) 28.

But most interest, at the press conference and later, focused on the introduction of the Congress resolutions. The *Glasgow Herald* of September 21st reported Sillars as saying that the "extremists would be effectively excluded by banning them".[2] Sillars said that he "would not feel able to defend the Kelvin resolution (if it were passed) by Congress". *The Scotsman* report confirmed the impression that the Kelvin resolution had been singled out for attack. It noted that Neil had "underlined Sillars' remarks when he said that the SLP would not be dominated by students or any group of Left-wing extremists".[3] Sillars subsequently justified his comments, and tried to head off the angry reaction they provoked in an interview granted

1. *Scotsman* 21st September 1976 page 6.
2. *Glasgow Herald* 21st September 1976 page 5.
3. *Scotsman* 21st September 1976 page 6.

to Bob Brown and published in the pre-Congress issue of the party's paper *Forward Scotland*. He said that the Kelvin resolution was inconsistent with the decisions of the Inaugural Meeting and with his subsequent statements based on those decisions.[4]

Kelvin, Cumbernauld and Stewarton branches wrote to the NOC. Cumbernauld's first point gives the tone of their objections:

> Comrades Sillars and Neil are condemned in the strongest possible terms for their personal utterances to the National Press which have seriously prejudged the Conference decisions."[5]

Not surprisingly, the NOC, at its meeting of October 9th, rejected this point. The NOC asked Cumbernauld not to take the matter to the national press as the branch had threatened.[6] The branch complied.

The September press conference raised the tension in the party. It re-awakened all the suspicions originally aroused at Darnley and Middleton Hall. It led the Cumbernauld branch to table an emergency resolution for the Congress instructing "that no national officer of the Party shall make personal statements to the press regarding Party business".[7] Further, it signalled that the leadership were determined to have out their fight with the dissidents, in public, at the Congress.

There can be no doubt that from this point to the Congress it was the NOC, not their enemies, who were spoiling for a fight. Cumbernauld, as we have seen, complied with a request not to publish its resolution. Kelvin, for its part also refused to make any comments to the press. It simply asked that Alex Neil or Jim Sillars come to a branch meeting to discuss the position. This request was refused. IMG, too, began to withdraw. At the September National Committee meeting the SLP was discussed and members, realising they might be expelled, moderated their position. Indeed, IMG moderated its position even more than the Kelvin and Cumbernauld branches. They agreed to press Kelvin to make its Resolution No. 41 merely advisory.[8]

In Scotland, IMG debated their position for the SLP Stirling Congress at both their September, and October meetings. By

4. *Forward Scotland* (Congress issue undated) page 1.
5. Letter by Cumbernauld branch signed by Bob McCabe. para. 1.
6. Minute of NOC 9th October page   1.
7. See below part II of this chapter.
8. See *Balance Sheet and Perspectives* Part II and *Resolutions on forthcoming SLP conference* passed by IMG SC para. 4.

September, it was clear to IMG that the positions they had staked out in June were not adequate. They had not been sufficiently precise in their political objectives and hence floundered about with different members supporting different positions. Some members, in Aberdeen, had supported STUC 17 — and helped to put it on the SLP Congress Agenda as Resolution No. 43, while others backed the Kelvin Resolution No. 41. This muddle divided their efforts and, they feared, increased outsiders' suspicisions of their intentions. This problem IMG sought to overcome by withdrawing their support for the Kelvin Resolution. They agreed, in September, to "focus an intervention into the Conference around uniting class struggle forces around opposition to the Government's policies . . . it would therefore be premature to make a general pragmatic intervention around policies like the Kelvin resolution".

The September 13th meeting of the Scottish Committee of IMG also reconsidered its position in relation to the rest of the SLP. While a raid for members was explicitly ruled out, the prospect of gaining new members for the IMG was in the wind. The SC Resolution of September on the SLP noted:

> The size of the forces now moving towards such a revolutionary regroupment means that Trotskyist forces would be a minority within it. . . . It may be necessary at some time in the *future* to urge withdrawal and fight for all revolutionary forces to affiliate to the Fourth International, but in the present relation of forces this would be unprincipled.[9]

The SC believed the whole SLP had turned left in an attempt to distinguish itself from the SNP. This perception raised IMG's hopes for the whole organisation, confirmed their own decision to join it, and increased their determination to work within the SLP.

IMG's problem all along was to be at once part of the SLP and to be distinguished from it. It needed to be part of the organisation to influence it and to make contact in it with potential recruits. It needed, at the same time, to be distinguished from it, to gain credit for whatever leftward shifts the SLP made and to give itself a public platform for its non-SLP activities. In September the SC resolved to try to comprise these two different positions by asking the SLP NOC to allow it to publicly set up an IMG tendency within the SLP.[10] A

9. *Resolution on the SLP* passed by IMG SC 13th September 1976 (as amended) para. 10. page 2.
10. *Op cit* Para. 35 Page 6.

less likely project is difficult to imagine.

At the following month's SC, IMG accepted the impossibility of any public declaration of their 'tendency' within the SLP. Defensively, the main Resolution at the October SC noted:

> . . . a witch-hunt by the leadership against revolutionary socialists would destroy the potential of the SLP. A party which accepted such a witch-hunt could not remain a credible force in the working class.[11]

It went on to urge its members to vote at the SLP Congress for Resolution 43 — which it considered most important — and several others. Unaware of these deliberations, the SLP NOC had a joint meeting, after its regular monthly meeting on the 9th of October, with the Party's Standing Orders Committee (SOC) to consider arrangements for the Stirling Congress. The SOC had four members: Litster Gardiner was its Secretary. The other members were John Macmillan (Chairman), Alan Morrison (Bonnybridge ex-SWRP and ex-IMG) and Andrew Noble (Paisley). Most of the SOC's report was uncontroversial enough. No mention of the IMG entry into the SLP was made.[12]

When the NOC and SOC reconvened for a further meeting on Saturday the 23rd of October — a week before the Congress — the position had been transformed. This time Gardiner, for the SOC, claimed that he had sufficient proof of IMG infiltration to demand the suspension from the Congress of the entire Leith Branch and seven named members of the IMG. The SOC wanted the members who were accused to prove that they were not members of IMG — for the SOC had no direct evidence that they were. What they did have however were two letters, one from Danny O'Hara, the Leith Branch secretary, and another from Tom Nairn of the Edinburgh South Branch, about the IMG infiltration. O'Hara's letter claimed that most of the members of the branch did not take part in branch activity and that the branch had fallen into the hands of three or four active members of the IMG. He suggested that it would therefore be dangerous to allow the Leith Branch to take part in Congress decisions. They should be allowed in as observers only. He did not name any of the people concerned.[13]

11. *Resolution on the forthcoming SLP Conference* proposed by Comrade Shevek Para. 6.
12. *Minute of NOC* 9th October 1976 Page 1.
13. This account of O'Hara's letter is based on interviews with Joe Farrell, Litster Gardiner, John Nairn, Margaret Mellis and Don Robertson.

When the relevant parts of O'Hara's letter were read to the October 23rd meeting, NOC member Mrs Margaret Mellis rejected it. Pointing out that O'Hara was the Secretary of the Branch and that it was a bit difficult to believe that he could not rally at least two or three other delegates along with himself and Gardiner (who was also a member of the Leith Branch) to outvote the IMG members, Mellis said that "the party had more to fear from infiltration from the right than the left".[14]

Gardiner also had a letter from Tom Nairn which was altogether more important than O'Hara's. Nairn had written to warn the party that IMG were planning to make an issue of the proposal, then being hotly debated, that a referendum be held on devolution. Nairn was scathing about IMG's position on this question. He pointed out that they were backing the referendum idea — then being proposed mainly by opponents of devolution because they thought a 'No' vote would triumph — because they could not make up their own minds about devolution. They were very suspicious of anything which looked like nationalism, and yet felt they would have to back it if the majority of the Scottish (or Welsh) people favoured the proposals. (This practice of backing a proposal which has popular support is known in the Trotskyist canon as 'Tailism' - it is a weak position in that the Trotskyist groups think of themselves as a vanguard.) Nairn informed the party that he had always thought that a confrontation with the IMG members of the SLP was inevitable, but that he was appalled and surprised to learn that they had decided to provoke a confrontation at this point. The SLP's IMG members were, he thought, too dumb and too impatient to practise 'entrism'. Nairn made it clear, in his letter, that he still hoped a confrontation at this time could be avoided, but his information from a London member of IMG was that it could not. IMG would fight on the Referendum issue and would also try to defeat the leadership on their pro-EEC stand. Whether IMG were too dumb to practise entrism is a nice point. My impression is that their real problem was that they were too divided to practise anything. I also have shown that IMG was — or, at any rate, thought it was — trying to withdraw from a confrontation with the leadership. Nairn's letters mentioned no names of IMG members, neither did it single out the Leith branch as a source of trouble.[15]

The SOC asked the NOC to take O'Hara's and Nairn's letter as

14. Interview with Margaret Mellis.
15. Letter of Tom Nairn made available to me by John Nairn (They are not related).

evidence of infiltration and as a reason for provoking a fight with the IMG. Yet Nairn's letter explicitly expressed the hope that a confrontation could be avoided and certainly was not intended to be a piece of evidence against the IMG. The names of the seven individuals whom the SOC's Special Report mentioned were obtained by hearsay. In the face of this 'evidence' and a threat by the SOC that it would resign if its proposed suspensions were not accepted, the NOC voted by fifteen votes to two to agree to the suspensions. The two who held out were Don Robertson and John Nairn. Pleas from them were brushed aside. Robertson specifically asked for a subcommittee of the NOC to consider the SOC report and to interview the indicted members and hear their side of the story. Their suggestion was rejected. Since the SOC had no evidence other than hearsay this was perhaps inevitable. Of course, harder evidence would have been very difficult to obtain. A confession from an IMG member would do, and certainly a recitation to the NOC of the evidence in the IMG documents on which I have based this study might have moved them, but the SOC lacked either of these kinds of support for their demand. In the midst of the argument at the NOC meeting Sillars uttered a remark which was to be heard more than once at the Congress — "At times of crisis, working class organisations expel without discussion". Sillars and Neil were intent on a public cleansing. One member of the NOC urged, "We should get our fucking pit boots on and wade right into them."[16] It was agreed to present the two SOC reports, the regular one and the Emergency Report agreed by the NOC on October 23rd, to the Congress separately. This was a small victory for John Nairn and Don Robertson as a combined Report would have passed Congress without any trouble. The separate Emergency Report might just be defeated.

Five days later, on Thursday, the day before the Congress began, the suspended members received a letter from Gardiner notifying them of the NOC's decision. The postal service will have to be improved in an independent Socialist Scotland. From this point there could be no withdrawal from confrontation at the Congress.

Unaware of these events, the Kelvin members met twice in the week before the Congress. On Tuesday the 26th of October a meeting of the ten member delegation to the Congress was held. Alan Freeman surprised those present by suggesting, in line with the IMG agreement to withdraw from a confrontation, that Resolution No. 41

16. Interview with Don Robertson and Margaret Mellis.

be retracted. He suggested that Kelvin move at Congress that the Resolution be referred to the incoming National Executive Committee (the draft Constitution which was to be approved at Stirling provided for the replacement of the NOC by an NEC of four officers and fifteen other members). Freeman's proposal was supported by Eve Oldham and Martin O'Leary. It was defeated by 7 votes to 3. A full meeting of the Kelvin Branch met on the following Thursday — the 28th — and heard the IMG case again. The full branch defeated the proposal as well. IMG won its way only after the branch had gone on to agree to move an emergency resolution calling for a special one-day Congress on EEC membership and urging that until then all resolutions bearing on the EEC should be considered indicative. Once this emergency resolution had been passed the Kelvin IMG members gleefully pointed out that Resolution 41 had implications for the EEC.[17] In the event the Stirling Congress was so disrupted by the suspension argument that Resolution No. 41 was never reached.

The NOC met on Friday afternoon before the Congress' first session which was held that evening. The main item of interest was, again, the IMG entry. The meeting had before it a two-page memorandum "The SLP: Entrism and Counter Measures" by Neal Ascherson, which he distributed to delegates. Ascherson had been elected to the NOC in the Spring but was an irregular attender. He had missed the October 23rd joint meeting with the SOC. His memorandum was a plea for compromise. Ascherson had learned of the Kelvin withdrawal, late the previous evening, understood its significance and confirmed his impression with "one of the (IMG's) most intelligent leaders in London". Ascherson's contact had been "horrified at the suggestion that IMG activity and the reaction to it might destroy the SLP". The trouble was laid at the door of "freelance leftists, of the 'cretinist' category (who) are causing much more trouble than actual IMG members or intimate sympathisers like Alan Freeman — who actually voted *against* the famous Kelvin Resolution in the branch". The SOC's suspensions, Ascherson suggested, were a mistake. "Several branches hostile on the whole to the far left have been appalled, and are likely to vote with the left against the platform on general grounds of intra-party democracy."

Ascherson's advice to his NOC colleagues was three-fold. Leading SLP members who proposed to resign if the suspensions were not

17. Kelvin Branch Minute of 28th October 1976 and interviews with Mackechnie, Cotter and Finn.

approved should make their position clear to the Congress. Secondly, an attempt should be made to divide the left by, say, lifting the suspension against the named IMG people and keeping it against the Leith Branch. Finally, "doubting delegations are entitled to hear the facts about anti-democratic or harmful episodes. If they don't they will remain suspicious of the SOC proposal".[18] It was too late. The NOC was not patient with advice from an irregular attender. It dismissed Ascherson's proposal on a motion of next business. There was no going back — confrontation it was to be.

When delegates arrived for the Congress they found copies of the Congress edition of *Forward Scotland*. Its main story was an interview by Bob Brown with Jim Sillars under the aptly dramatic head "It's Make or Break". To Brown's question "How important is the first Congress?" Sillars answered in the terms in which the Congress, and to a real extent, the party, would be judged:

> J.S.: "It's critical, it's make or break for the SLP. Nobody is going to support or join us because we're nice people who mean well. They will support us only if we produce policies they recognise to be relevant to their needs and aspirations. . . . But there is another crucial aspect of the Congress — to establish beyond doubt the principles on which the SLP will function, a democratic party with an accountable leadership."[19]

So it was to be.

II

The SOC had planned three sessions for the Congress. On Friday evening in private session, the party would (a) approve a constitution; (b) agree to Standing Orders, and (c) agree branch guidelines. On Saturday morning, the plan called for debates on (a) Scottish Government, (b) Local Government, and (c) Patronage. Saturday afternoon was to begin with a private session on party finance. This was to be followed by a public session with debates on Education, Housing, Pensions and Social Security, and Foreign Policy. Sunday was to be about "Jobs and Industry" and "Land Policy" on which the party had issued important policy documents. There were also to be discussions of Energy and Oil Policy,

18. Ascherson, "The SLP: Entrism and Counter-Measures". Ascherson distributed a half dozen photocopies at the meeting. Interviews with Robertson, Ascherson, John Nairn and Joe Farrell.
19. *Forward Scotland* (Congress issue undated) Page 1.

Transport, Fishing, Social Services, Minorities, and Political Education.

Joe Farrell was in the Chair for the Friday evening. After the formalities of introduction, the Congress moved to consider the Special SOC Report on suspensions. The party was meeting behind closed doors in private session. As soon as Litster Gardiner rose to speak to the Special Report, the journalists waiting outside could hear the mood of the Congress change. It was, as one of them remembered, more like a football match than a political debate. In many ways the proceedings were a replay of the NOC-SOC discussion of the same issue on October 23rd. But this time no evidence was produced at all. Gardiner did, however, allude to Tom Nairn's letter. There can be no doubt that the fact that the letter came from a man with such impeccable left-wing credentials helped the SOC proposal.[20] (Tom Nairn did not arrive at the Congress until Saturday and so was unable to explain his position which, as we have seen, was to avoid confrontation). Delegates who were present have told me that they think about a third of the meeting was opposed to the suspensions. But the Congress was cowed into submission by threats of resignation from both the party's MPs if the SOC Special Report was not approved.[21] They won the card vote on this report by 569 votes to 212 with 11 abstentions. Branches had one vote for each member. They could — and did — split their votes. The rage which many felt when the votes were announced played an important part in the crisis which came to a head on Sunday morning. But this rage was not apparent at the time. Don Robertson told me that the NOC members sitting near him were relieved because they thought they had won.[22] The rest of Friday evening's proceedings passed amicably enough and it was possible for the leadership to believe that their 'public cleansing' strategy had worked.

There were three debates of interest on the Constitution. The NOC mostly had its way. The liveliest debate was on the dual membership rule. The draft Constitution had proposed, at Clause III No. 2, that:

> Members of other organisation and parties that promote distinctive political aims exclude themselves from membership of the SLP.

Stirling Branch proposed an amendment:

20. Interviews with Don Robertson, Ian Millar and Carol Craig.
21. *Scotsman* 30th October 1976 Page 1.
22. Interview with Don Robertson.

As the Scottish Labour Party presents itself as the main Socialist movement in Scotland, membership is open to all Socialists in agreement with Clause 2 of the present constitution.[23]

This amendment was defeated by a show of hands. Thus the NOC's invocation of a 'dual-membership' rule was backed by Congress. Congress also remitted after a debate, a proposal from Glasgow University Branch that a special meeting of the party's new National Council could be called by 50% of the branches. The main objection to the proposal seemed to be that the proportion — 50% — was too high. An amendment from Aberdeen proposing that branches should have final say in the selection of Parliamentary candidates was also defeated. However, Congress did pass an amendment from Kelvin allowing the final say to the newly established National Council.

The Constitution stated four objects for the new party. Firstly, the party was committed to the creation of a Scottish Parliament "working in full democratic partnership and on an equal basis with other nations within and outwith the British Isles".[24] Ambiguous though it was, this was a stronger "devolutionary" stance than the party had been committed to previously. The Party moved more and more to the SNP's position on the Scottish question as time passed. The hardening of the Labour Party's view made this necessary. Ambiguously, too, the party committed itself to attempting to secure "for the people in Scotland independent representation in European institutions and other appropriate international institutions". This is "Scotland in Europe" the now familiar shibboleth — without mention of the EEC. The party was committed thirdly to democratic socialism and finally to working closely with "the democratic organisations of the labour and trade union movements both within and outwith the British Isles". Socialism had become a tepid last.

Membership — excluding members of other parties — was open to all over the age of 16. It was not restricted to Scots. Half of the membership fee was to be retained by the members' branch: half was to go to the central organisation. Membership was to cost OAPs 50p; everyone else would pay £1.[25] This was a reduction of 50% from the fee demanded until October. Repeated attempts by Sillars and Neil to have such a change made earlier by the NOC had been rejected. The effect on the party's central organisation would be a cut from £2

23. SLP Edinburgh Branch — *November Bulletin*.
24. Constitution Clause II.
25. Constitution Clause III.

107

per member in 1976 to 50p per member thereafter — since the centre received all the dues in 1976.

The basic unit of party organisation was to be the branch. Branches were to be based — in the manner of the SNP — on places of residence, work or study. Labour Party individual membership is based on place of residence alone. No mention of trade union affiliation was made. Each branch would have two members on a National Council (NC). Members of the NEC and officers would also be members of the NC. The NC would draw up policy documents and consider appeals from decisions of the NEC. It would also draw up any party manifestos. Normally, it would meet twice a year.[26] This provision mirrors the SNP constitution.

The supreme body in the party would be the Congress which would meet each October. Branches would appoint representatives to the Congress. Congress would have the power to agree to — or reject — the NC's policy statements. It would elect the chairmen of the party's Scottish Assembly, Westminster and European Parliamentary groups.[27] It would also elect an NEC of 15 Ordinary members and the party Chairman, Executive Chairman, Vice-Chairman, and Treasurer every year. The General Secretary, an *ex officio* member of the NEC, would be elected every four years. The NEC was to be the effective organiser of the party and in charge of its money. It would also appoint a Constitutional Commission which would keep the Constitution under review.

The Draft was largely acclaimed by the Congress, once the SOC report had been approved on Friday night. Ascherson could quote Neil, on the front page of Saturday's *Scotsman*, saying of the vote on the Special SOC Report '. . .This was the decision on what sort of party we are going to be —an ultra-leftist one based on the IMG, or a mainstream left-of-centre party".[28] Ascherson estimated in the *Scotsman* that there were "never more than 20 IMG people in the SLP".[29] His paper for the NOC the previous evening had said that IMG and their sympathisers in the SLP "can't exceed 60 or 70". But since they were now thought to be out, perhaps the exact figure no longer mattered. Ascherson further reported that the SLP delegates were "still a little dizzy from the poll prediction in The *Scotsman* yesterday — that 28% of Labour voters would consider switching to

26. Constitution Clauses IV, V and VIII.
27. Constitution Clause VI.
28. *Scotsman* 30th October 1976 page 1.
29. *Scotsman* 30th October, 1976, page.5.

the SLP". This ORC poll for the *Scotsman* was unique. It asked voters, after they had declared their preference, if they would consider switching to the SLP. (Prompted answers of this kind can be depended upon to produce a highly favourable rate of answers and are therefore of little value.) Doubly buoyed by an encouraging opinion poll and by suspending the Leith Branch and the named IMG members, the party looked forward to Saturday.

On Saturday morning, the business went smoothly. The most controversial resolution was from Stewarton Branch. It called upon the party: "To adopt a policy of independence for Scotland and to seek to promote a Scottish Socialist Workers' Republic."[30] This was the SWRP position. Indeed, its presence on the list of printed resolutions had embarrassed the SWRP-run Bonnybridge Branch, since they felt Stewarton had stolen a march on them. They hoped to recoup some of this ground by putting down an amendment which called on the party to "adopt a policy of Socialist independence for Scotland".[31] The amendment was a moderately worded version of the original resolution. Stewarton's delegates accepted it because, among other reasons, the press campaign against their resolution made it impossible to discuss it in a calm atmosphere.[32] Congress passed the amended resolution. This debate and the subsequent debate on a resolution from Paisley, raised the European issue. Paisley's resolution — suitably composited — read:

> This Congress resolves that a Scottish Parliament be set up with all the necessary powers required to create a Socialist Scotland including the right to legislate over the oil companies and to raise taxation on oil brought ashore in Scotland.

> Moreover, as the move to political unity in Europe proceeds, Congress further resolves that all steps be taken by the UK Parliament to prepare and enact the constitutional changes necessary to obtain for Scotland full representation proportional with other countries at all levels in the EEC.[33]

The 'platform' position was to accept British membership of the EEC and fight a two-stage campaign for 'Scotland in Europe'. The first stage would be during devolution when Scotland would be represented as part of the UK in the EEC institutions (i.e. as at

30. Scottish Government Composite page 3.
31. Interview with Norman Easton.
32. *Ibid.*
33. Amendment to Congress Resolution. page 5.

present). The second stage would involve direct representation for Scotland in the EEC.

Success for the NOC on this Resolution by 549 votes for, to 178 votes against, may have suggested that the Left would cause no further trouble on the European issue.[34] But this was not to be. Throughout the day, particularly in the afternoon, speakers could draw loud acclamation from the Congress by attacking the Common Market. For example, Douglas Gilchrist, a teacher from Cumbernauld, drew applause by suggesting that the party's policy on Europe needed a third stage — withdrawal from the EEC. This unnerved the Leadership given, on the one hand Sillars' long commitment to 'Scotland in Europe' and, on the other, their knowledge, confirmed by Tom Nairn's letter, that the Left would try to beat them on this issue.

Still, on the surface, the NOC had its way with the Congress on most matters. Hamilton's resolution asking for greater emphasis in party propaganda on the SLP's role in UK politics was passed on a show of hands. The platform won, although more narrowly, a card vote on the issue of proportional representation. Here the Congress backed the principle of P.R. by a mere 469 votes for to 316 votes against.[35] The strong vote against the platform on this issue is intriguing for it can only be explained as a carry-over to the SLP of the Labour Party's old aversion to P.R. The Labour Party would have much to lose to parties like the SLP should such a system be adopted.

On Saturday afternoon, the platform lost a vote on a show of hands. A resolution from Glasgow University branch called on Congress to reject the arms race, the production and export of arms, the militaristic bias of the media, and committed the SLP to fight for:

1. Unilateral nuclear disarmament
2. Withdrawal from NATO.
3. The transfer of resources from military to peaceful production and a Government ban on, and TU blacking of, all military equipment (including spare parts), for export to South Africa, Chile, Israel and the Arab States as a first step towards this.[36]

It also called for a boycott of South African trade. Against the advice of the NOC — who were by this time running out of speakers and repeating themselves — Congress approved this resolution by an

34. Correspondence with Sheila Gilmour (NEC Member).
35. *Ibid.*
36. Resolution No. 29.

110

H

overwhelming show of hands. But the most interesting, and portentous decisions on Saturday afternoon concerned a series of emergency resolutions which had been tabled during the morning. The procedure — a fairly normal one for a Congress of this type — was for the SOC to consider the emergency resolutions and make recommendations on them to the Congress. The use of emergency resolutions to raise issues which the platform does not wish discussed is also normal. For a group out of favour with the platform the procedure is often preferrable to putting down ordinary resolutions, because it allows the platform less time to prepare its response. Dissident groups use the device when they suspect that they are more in tune with the feelings of a meeting than the platform. The device was fully used at the Stirling Congress.

The SOC was confronted with four emergency resolutions. Three were from Kelvin. The first asked for a special one-day Congress to discuss the EEC and requested that until this Congress took place, all votes which had implications for the EEC should be considered indicative. This, of course, was the emergency resolution which had allowed the IMG members of Kelvin branch to retreat on Resolution No. 41. The second was similar to the first, differing only in wording. Its submission along with the first was caused by an oversight. Kelvin's third resolution concerned the cuts. It called upon the Congress to reassert:

> . . . its total opposition to the Labour Government's cuts in social expenditure. In this light it opposes with greater determination the proposed cuts which we are starting to receive. . . .
> It
> 1. Calls on the NEC to organise a one-day Conference with all interested trade union, political and other organisations within the next month.
> 2. Pledges its support to activities against the cuts.
> 3. Calls on the NEC to instruct the Secretary to circulate the branches with information he receives from other areas so that branches can get a complete national overview.[37]

Although the three Kelvin resolutions called for action and policies which were anathema to the leaders none of them posed a direct threat. This was not true of the fourth emergency resolution, from Cumbernauld. An adaptation of the branch's earlier letter to the NOC, it read:

> This Congress, in view of recent events, instructs that no National

37. Emergency Resolution on Local Government.

111

Officer of the Party shall make unauthorised personal statements to the press regarding Party business.

Cumbernauld were hoping that the point made by the Stewarton delegate about press interference would influence delegates to approve this part of the resolution. It concluded:

> Further, that in future, no prior notice of the Congress Agenda shall be released to the Press until it has been circulated, discussed and amended by Party branches. Only the final Agenda for Congress shall be issued to the Press.[38]

The SOC reported, reasonably enough, that it could not accept that any of the emergency resolutions was about an 'emergency'. Then it tried to forestall debate on any of them by insisting that Congress vote to discuss either all or none of them. Eric Davidson (East Kilbride), who had a local government job which was threatened by the cuts, and Lindsay Paterson (Aberdeen), argued strongly for a debate on Kelvin's third resolution. Gardiner acknowledged his own sympathy with the 'cuts' resolution but stuck to his Committee's line — all the emergency resolutions or none; and he wanted none.[39] On behalf of Kelvin, Gerry Finn then offered to withdraw the first two resolutions. Finn took the opportunity to score a few points for Kelvin. They were, he said, agreeing to withdraw the two resolutions because the Congress had had a full opportunity to debate EEC membership and Kelvin acknowledged that it had been in error to bring up the matter again.[40] The SOC strategy was then in ruins. Congress voted to debate the third and fourth resolutions.

Soon after this the SOC reported back that they could still not accept that a debate should take place on the Cumbernauld Resolution, but allocated time for the debate on the Kelvin (cuts) Resolution at the end of Saturday afternoon. The SOC agreed to meet with Cumbernauld to discuss the position. Richard Cotter moving the Kelvin Resolution set out the effects that the cuts would have in Strathclyde Region. The only criticisms of the resolution were about the timing of the proposed conference, and the problem of financing the campaign. Sillars then declared his support for the resolution, but he asked the Kelvin delegation to trust him on its timing; their proposal for a conference next month was impractical.

38. Emergency Resolution.
39. Interview with Ian Millar (NEC member).
40. Interview with Gerry Finn.

Congress then voted unanimously for the Kelvin Resolution. (The Conference was never held.)

Finally, the Congress turned its attention to the Cumbernauld Emergency Resolution. The SOC and the Cumbernauld Branch could not agree about it. The SOC had offered to remove its objection if Cumbernauld would drop the first sentence of its resolution, but Cumbernauld was unmoved by the offer. Now the shoe was on the other foot. Having asked the Congress to the Emergency Resolutions together the platform had landed itself with the third and fourth, whereas it might have otherwise had to deal only with the third. Several delegates came to the rostrum to say that they had voted for both only in order to get the third. Cumbernauld were not giving way however. Bob McCabe, one of their delegation, made the point that the Congress had already voted to discuss their resolution. It should not go back on its own democratically arrived at decisions. The heated debate which followed did not go well for the platform. Eventually, the Chairman, Danus Skene, asked if the Congress would let Sillars speak, as he wanted to make his position clear on this issue. A number of 'Nos' rang out at what some took to be an attempt to dictate to the Congress. One woman from the Ayr Branch shouted 'Dictator' at Sillars. He stormed off the platform.[41] The Congress now had the bit in its teeth, and voted — for the second time — to debate the Cumbernauld Resolution. The debate was set for the first item of business on Sunday morning. The session concluded on time despite the debates on the emergency resolutions.

Clearly, the opposition to the platform could not be attributed to the IMG. They had — or so the SOC told the NOC — been suspended. No, opposition was no longer confined to IMG and a few sympathetic delegates — it was growing. Here the fact that the 'intellectual' branches had taken up their full quota of delegates made a difference because these were the delegates from which the opposition came. Their speakers were also more experienced. It is not surprising that the leaders were alarmed.

They were alarmed too by the news which trickled back to them of a meeting in the Station Hotel during the lunch break that day. The meeting had been called by delegates who were unhappy about the suspensions. Its purpose was to decide what line to take about this decision. The meeting was chaired by Jim Mackechnie and was attended by a number of NOC members such as Jim Young, John Nairn and Margaret Mellis. About eighty delegates plus about

41. Interview with Margaret Mellis.

twenty or so others including the suspended members attended this meeting. It is worth mentioning that this was the first attempt of the anti-leadership forces (aside, of course, from the IMG members) to work together. They decided to recommend that the suspended delegates appeal against the decision.[42] Then at the end of the meeting they decided, in response to a request from an Edinburgh delegate, to vote for a slate of candidates for the NEC — but many of the delegations had already cast their votes. This group had conferred as a result of the bullying and emotional threats from the platform. Their meeting resulted in more bullying. Those at the Station Hotel meeting formed the nucleus of the group which was to be thrown out of the party on Sunday.

Without doubt, the Congress had not gone well for Sillars and Neil. One delegate had informed the delegates late on the Saturday afternoon that he was really proud of the new party. Here at last was a party in which decisions were taken by Congress and not behind closed doors. This came in the midst of the debate on the emergency resolutions. But although Kelvin and Cumbernauld won the Congress' votes, they may also have alienated the many Ayrshire delegates. There was much rather obvious resentment at the way speaker after speaker came from Kelvin or Cumbernauld and at the way they used the emergency resolution procedure to humble the leaders. On the other hand, some delegations, like those from Edinburgh and Dundee, were reassured by the Kelvin people.[43] Certainly, they were not the wild men which the advance publicity had portrayed. The truth is that the party which had been so hastily and so emotionally cobbled together was beginning to come apart at the seams. In addition, the Kelvin and Cumbernauld delegations, supported by the East coast cities, were gaining control from the Ayrshire delegations and the leaders.

But the leadership continued to meet and plan after the end of the Saturday afternoon session. By 5.30 Danus Skene had come down to the hotel foyer to inform amused delgates that Alex Neil had upstaged Jim Sillars for once. Neil was resigning. Early in the evening most of the delegates went to a social. Skene, who had been in the Chair for much of the Saturday afternoon, was trying to convince some delegates from the Edinburgh and Dundee branches that he had evidence of a conspiracy between Kelvin and Cumbernauld. The Kelvin delegation had gone home for the

42. Interview with Jim Mackechnie.
43. Interview with Ray Chalmers (Dundee) and Carol Craig.

evening. Most of the Cumbernauld delegation were elsewhere in Stirling, having a Chinese dinner. They did not return to the hotel until about ten. In the meantime, the arguments in the hotel became bitter and intense.[44] As Neal Ascherson was to put it in the *Scotsman*, "A grim evening ensued with knots of delegates violently quarrelling into the small hours."[45] Pressure was applied to the delegates thought to be in the middle between the leadership and the Kelvin-Cumbernauld position. At this point members of the platform party began to elaborate what came to be known as the 'pincer-theory'. The first arm of the pincer was the Kelvin Emergency Resolution on the cuts. It was seen as a clever ploy to get the party committed to a campaign on the cuts. Point 3 of the Kelvin Resolution was cited as a particularly devious ploy to commit all the party's resources to the campaign. The second arm of the pincer was the Cumbernauld Resolution. This would gag the MPs — or rather tie them to the NOC. The net result, it was asserted, would have been to give IMG power beyond their wildest dreams. It would control the party apparatus and would have two MPs. Implicit in this 'theory' was the notion that Kelvin and Cumbernauld were IMG controlled and that they could control the Congress and the NOC. Somebody was having wild dreams alright.

At about 11.00 Sillars and Neil appeared at the social. Their previous absence had been noticed but not dwelt on. Only John Robertson remained above the fray. At one stage he and his partner did a lone quickstep on the dance floor. Sillars and Neil increased the pressure on the delegates in the middle. Edinburgh delegates were accused of being 'yellow' and 'chicken livered'. They were suspected of having supported the two emergency resolutions. Ascherson's description for Tuesday's *Scotsman* (which defended the leaders) admitted:

> . . .the platform, in putting the heat on the bewildered delegates in the middle, also argued that "the working class way" is to suspend all the rules in an emergency and display total, unquestioning loyalty to every move the Leadership makes until the crisis is over.[46]

That was the line.

It is possible that the Leadership panicked at a piece of evidence that was never produced at the Congress: the ballot for the new NEC.

44. Interview with Ian Millar.
45. *Scotsman* 1st November 1976, page 1.
46. *Scotsman* 2nd November 1976 page 11.

The expelled delegates charged that the balloting had resulted in several victories for them. If true this would help to explain the implicit premise in the 'pincer' story. No evidence of any cheating has ever been produced. But the Leadership left themselves wide open to the charge. The Congress had elected tellers on Friday. They were Terry Finlayson, Joe Handy, Jimmy Frame, Paul McDonald, Eric Davidson and Carol Craig.[47] But unknown to the Congress the SOC took it upon themselves to appoint a Chief Teller. He was Alan Morrison. As Morrison was a candidate himself this was not the wisest choice. As he came top of the poll the appointment was doubly unfortunate. Further, at least one elected teller — Carol Craig — was not allowed to see the ballots. It is not even clear when the ballots were counted.

Later that night at a meeting in Alex Neil's room in the Golden Lion Hotel a rump of the exhausted and confused NOC resumed their discussions and decided to expel 'the troublemakers'.[48] Four branches, Kelvin, Cumbernauld, Stirling and Stirling University were singled out for expulsion. The weapon chosen was an emergency resolution in the name of Ayr, seconded by East Kilbride:

> Congress calls for the immediate disbandment of the Kelvin, Cumbernauld, Stirling and Stirling University branches of the Scottish Labour Party and for the expulsion forthwith of those responsible for disrupting the proceedings of Congress.[50]

The rump of the NOC agreed to allow discussion of the motion, though the already well worn resignation threats were to be part of the argument.

On Sunday morning, when the Congress reassembled, there was elaborate stage-management but no debate. When the delegates arrived rumours of resignations were flying around. The Cumbernauld Emergency Resolution was on the delegates' seats. Before the meeting could begin the press were asked to leave. This was to be a private session. New Stewards — not those elected by the Congress — were very much in evidence. Once delegates were in the main room they were not allowed to leave for any reason. Delegates noticed important empty places on the platform. Had Neil and Sillars resigned? They were not to be seen. Curtains were drawn across the doors so that no one could look in. Joe Farrell took the Chair. Several times he announced that he was waiting for additional

47. Standing Orders reports.
48. Interview with David McMurran.
50. Emergency Resolution — Ayr and East Kilbride.

members. Finally ready, he announced that everyone who had a right to be there, was there (Neil and Sillars were not). The first item of business, he announced, was the Cumbernauld Emergency Resolution, but before that there was another Resolution. The party had come to the crossroads, he proclaimed.

Gardiner then read out the Ayr-East Kilbride Emergency Resolution. Only then did the stewards distribute it. Gardiner's recitation of the motion was greeted by a roar from the delegates. Misled by this shout into thinking that he didn't need to allow discussion, Farrell moved directly to the vote. In fact, many delegates hardly knew what was happening.[51] Perhaps the 'roar' which moved Farrell away from the agreement for a debate was exaggerated in his ears by the fact that the Ayrshire delegates tended to sit up front. In any case he put the matter immediately to the vote and won by 516 votes for to 271 against.[52] The vote was followed by scenes of truly black emotion. The four expelled branches were furious. It was a miracle that fighting did not break out. Many of the idealistic younger delegates were completely unprepared for what was happening.

The disbanded branches and all or part of eighteen other branches left the Golden Lion Hotel and set themselves up at the Station Hotel where, claiming to be the real SLP, they set up an alternative Congress. John Nairn was elected Chairman. They agreed to hold a reconvened Congress, in Stirling, in two weeks. The IMG delegates were among this group.[53]

Back in the Golden Lion Hotel the planned order of business was scrapped. Sillars and Neil who had joined the meeting left again in a huff after shouts of 'Dictator' greeted Sillars. The Chair was taken by John Robertson. Even here, after the suspension of the Leith Branch and the named IMG delegates, plus the loss of eighty or so others including all of at least four branches, the leadership was still in trouble.

By this point it was abundantly clear that the Congress had been a disastrous failure in precisely the way Sillars had asked it to be judged. It had not reached, and patently was not going to reach, any decision on the central 'Jobs and Industry' document. It had agreed to a rather backhanded resolution on the Common Market — but the Congress was plainly unhappy about its decision. It had agreed,

51. Interview with Joe Farrell.
52. *Scotsman* 2nd November 1976 page 1.
53. Interview with John Nairn.

117

without even a vote being taken, to an extreme position on disarmament and withdrawal from NATO, which was anything but 'mainstream Socialist' and would have been impossible for Sillars to defend. More important than this the party had been bullied and blackmailed by its leaders in the process of throwing out the IMG members. *Forward Scotland* had posed the crisis facing the Congress as "make or break". By Sunday afternoon it had not been 'make'.

Indeed in one sense an historical account of the SLP ends with the expulsion of the four branches on Sunday morning, October 31st. The history of the party covers a mere ten months. For at this point the party had lost its self-respect and its claim to stand for anything other than self-preservation. Neal Ascherson's defence of the expulsions in the following Tuesday's *Scotsman* unwittingly gave the game away:

> . . . how far can a party tolerate organised dissenting groups, even when they are not an 'entry' from outside? No real answer exists. Ironically, the IMG themselves have, or rather, have in theory, a high degree of internal democracy: the various 'Tendencies' each formulate their own general policy platforms, and are then proportionally represented in the Leadership. They do not, however, fight elections. And as long as it is accepted that a party must present a "united front" to be credible with voters, the pressure for conformity of belief will remain.[54]

And the *Economist's* reporter observed:

> The party, which broke from Labour last December in protest at Labour's reluctance to offer home rule to Scotland, never looked like lasting more than a few years. The ferocious way in which last weekend's expulsions took place may have accelerated its decline. . . . Even so the party can count on plenty of publicity north of the border (it is the darling of the Scottish political correspondents) . . . those that live by the splinter, die by the splinter.[55]

III

The record of the SLP after Sunday's expulsions is a record of a somnambulist. Though the party had too much energy to lie down and die, it did not regain conscious direction. In the few hours after the expulsions when Alex Neil and Jim Sillars were packing their bags to leave, John Robertson revealed wholly unexpected powers as

54. *Scotsman* 2nd November, page 11.
55. *Economist* 6th November 1976 page 27.

118

a medical miracle man. He rallied the patient to the extent of its regaining the will to live. He had no help from Neil or Sillars. They reappeared at the Congress and denounced the delegates for lacking "guts and acumen" and for failing to support them. It was a repeat, before a larger audience, of the sentiments expressed the previous evening at the social.

Neil again announced his resignation. Not for the first time he took a harder line than Sillars. At a lunch time meeting, Sillars told the press that he would rejoin the party only if it showed that it had sufficient character. If it defeated a new emergency resolution now before Congress in the name of the Dundee branches by a margin of two to one, he would be back. The Dundee Resolution had condemned the Chair for its handling of the expulsions and demanded a right of appeal against the expulsion. As it was Congress, or what remained of it, only defeated the new resolution by a margin of 230 votes for to 377 against. Still, somehow, Sillars could take this, and the party's subsequent vote to carry on, as a sufficient basis for him to return and be the Chairman of what he called a "reborn" party.

Chapter VII:

The Aftermath

After the fracas at Stirling there were two organisations claiming to be the SLP. There was the 'official' organisation behind Jim Sillars and Alex Neil. And there was the loose collection of expelled branches and individuals who sympathised with them, grouped around John Nairn, the Cumbernauld branch and eventually the Scottish Aggregate of IMG. Individual members of IMG who had escaped the expulsions at Stirling were thrown out by their branches under the dual membership rule and most of them, as well as a good many IMG members who had not been in the SLP, joined with their expelled comrades. As the history of the latter group, the SLP (DW i.e. Democratic Wing as it called itself) is the shorter I will look at it first.

The SLP (DW) met on Sunday afternoon after the expulsions and agreed from the first to claim to be the legitimate heir to the whole organisation. Their claim was based on the unconstitutionality, as they saw it, of the Sunday expulsions. From their point of view the actions taken by the Congress up to Sunday morning were considered valid and they proceeded on this basis. There is some irony here. The SLP (DW) — the "Breakaway-Breakaway", as they were immediately dubbed — objected to the platform's procedures, particularly at the Congress on the Sunday, on much the same grounds that Sillars and Neil had originally objected to the Labour Party. Their charge of "unconstitutionality" was analogous to Sillars' early claim of 'broken promises'. This similarity is no accident, of course — both were basing their charge on the strict literalism of the British left.[1]

As a stop-gap measure to help them organise their party they established a seven-person Steering Committee of John Nairn (Chairman, Cumbernauld), Sean Tierney (Kelvin), Margaret Mellis (Dunfermline), Martin Syme (St Andrews), Corry McChord (Stirling), Chris Bamberry (Leith and Edinburgh) and Pat Kane (Aberdeen). This was one member from each branch of which they had a majority. That their position was in truth untenable was never denied. They saw four options available to them:

(a) Reconciliation: This could be accomplished only if some serious indication of a major change of heart from the Sillars camp was forthcoming. Some of the members who remained with Sillars, particularly in the Edinburgh and Dundee branches, hoped to effect a reconciliation.

(b) Create a Separate Party: This could only be a very long-term proposition — but was not impossible. The SLP (DW) had many more members than any of the other parties on the far Left and might well have hoped for further recruits from disaffected members of the SLP in branches which had stayed in the Party.

(c) Federal Structure: This option was thought to have the advantages of both (a) and (b). But like (a), would have required major concessions from the other SLP. The members of the SLP (DW) thought that other branches of the SLP might be attracted to this idea.

(d) Return to the Labour Party: This made sense as an option for the SLP (DW) only as a threat against the SLP. It would have demonstrated the hollowness of the charge that they were Left wing extremists.[2]

None of these options really made much sense unless the SLP (DW) could attract numbers of members away from the SLP. In order not to discourage such potential recruits they maintained the ban on the Leith Branch and the seven named IMG members.

This decision was reluctantly accepted — for the time being — by the IMG members of the SLP (DW). It suited them to show the non-IMG members just how reasonable they were. But reasonable or not, their presence was much more numerically significant in the SLP (DW) than ever it had been in the SLP. If Gardiner and his SOC thought that they had to get rid of the IMG because they were too numerous for the small SLP to control, this was even more of a problem for the SLP (DW). The truth is that the SLP (DW) was split

1. Interview with John Nairn.
2. Interview with Gerry Finn.

121

from the beginning against itself. It had two groups of members — the IMG and the others. IMG had numerous advantages in the fight for control of the organisation. They were known to each other, had well-established channels of communication, and could be depended upon to turn up at the SLP (DW) meetings. None of these things was true of the other members.

Both groups realised, however, that the battle between them was going to be won by the group that could bring in the most recruits from the outside. IMG brought in its Scottish members one by one — and the others dropped out in the same way. But before this could happen the SLP (DW) held its reconvened Congress. The Congress was held in Stirling on November 14th. It passed three Emergency Resolutions. The first was from Cumbernauld and blamed the damage to the SLP on its leaders and the NOC. It asked for an SLP (DW) with a strong branch basis. It passed a resolution from the expelled members of the Aberdeen branch calling for a further conference on policy in January and giving sanction to the decision in the Station Hotel to set up a National Council. The reconvened Congress also passed the Cumbernauld Emergency Resolution on statements to the press by party officers which had been the subject of such heat on the afternoon of Saturday, October 30th. Finally, it persuaded the Leith branch to withdraw its resolution which asked for its suspension to be lifted. This was the last meeting of the SLP (DW) before the IMG took over.

From this point the non-IMG branches were playing for time, hoping they could draw enough additional support into the Party to keep IMG from taking over. With this in view it was decided not to meet again before January on the grounds that the Party should go all out to help arrange a rally after an STUC organised demonstration on the public expenditure cuts. The SLP (DW) tried to organise a meeting with other branches. A meeting arranged in a public hall in Kirkcaldy between John Nairn, Don Robertson (representing Fife), Gerry Finn (of the Kelvin Branch), Ian Millar (a member of the new NEC and a delegate from Edinburgh South), Dougie Bathie (Kelvin — and before that a founder member of the Airdrie and Coatbridge branch), Ray Chalmers (of Dundee Central branch) and Tom Nairn came to nothing. The non-IMG part of the party could not be organised.[3] Its members had too little in common. A revulsion against both Sillars and the IMG was not enough.

For its part IMG suffered no such problems. I am told that Ernest

3. Interview with John Nairn, Don Robertson, Gerry Finn and Ian Millar.

Mandel, the political theorist and General Secretary of the Fourth International, came to Glasgow to see for himself and advise his Scottish Comrades. He urged them to stay in the SLP (DW). They didn't need much encouragement. The NC of IMG resolved, in early November, to:

> urge its supporters in Scotland to attempt to establish and build the SLP (DW).[4]

The resolution was carried almost unanimously. The NC further resolved to allow "IMG members in Scotland to leave the IMG and the FI and not to have national and international democratic centralism". On the other hand such 'ex'-members were to "move as rapidly as possible to ask the SLP (DW) for the right of membership of the FI". There was no possibility the SLP (DW) would invoke the dual-membership rule — even though it had been agreed to before the split — because of the way it had been abused by the Stirling Congress. In addition, IMG's decision of November meant that Scottish Comrades had ceased to be members of the IMG. Without such protection IMG dominance, once IMG had decided to enter, was inevitable.

This dominance made itself felt on January 29th, 1977, at the SLP (DW) first National Council meeting which was held in the City Halls, Glasgow. The non-IMG branches reported little activity. Glasgow Kelvin "had not discussed a political programme". Cumbernauld had "maintained their strength". Stirling branch did not attend. The IMG branches, on the other hand, were full of activity. A Paisley branch had been established and held a public meeting. The Aberdeen branch had set up alongside a strong SLP branch and was holding a meeting on local issues. A South Glasgow branch had been formed and in Edinburgh a single branch of the SLP (DW) had been formed out of the three previously active SLP branches (Leith, North-Central and South).[5]

The IMG delegates who declared their formation of a 'Fourth International Tendency' were convinced that Sillars' SLP had ceased trying to be a Socialist organisation and would soon join hands with the SNP. Partly for this reason they believed they should no longer shelter behind the now confused name "SLP (DW)", but should set up a new organisation. These ideas were embodied in a resolution from the Aberdeen branch — which also called for another

4. 'Mills. J.' *Resolutions for Scottish Aggregate* (November, 1976).
5. *Minute of the SLP (Democratic Wing) National Council Meeting No. 1.* pp. 1-2.

Conference within six weeks. It passed unanimously.

Sensing what was going on the non-IMG members in Kelvin had to fight even to disband their own branch. Kelvin ceased to be a branch of the SLP (DW) at its next meeting on February 3rd. Cumbernauld wound itself up on February 12th. On March 12th and 13th the remains of the SLP (DW) were transformed into the Scottish Socialist League (SSL). The SSL consisted of the Scottish members of IMG, those English members of the IMG who were colonising Scotland, and some recruits. It wanted to affiliate to the Fourth International. IMG was well on the way to achieving Sillars' goal of 'Scotland in Europe' for itself.

II

If, for their part, the SLP (DW) and its IMG 'ex'-members in particular, accused Sillars of abandoning 'socialism' in favour of 'nationalism', the most even-tempered statement of the SLP's position turned this charge upside down. Tom Nairn, in a two-page broadsheet to his Edinburgh fellow members, accused the Left of not ever really taking nationalism seriously. The broadsheet was called 'The National Question'. It asserted that:

> The SLP was founded on the assumption that the questions of socialism and nationalism were about equally important in terms of strategy. A new, distinctly left-wing socialism would give meaning to self-government; but, also, a breakthrough in the area of national self-rule would provide the new opportunity for socialism. . . . We have to fight coherently on both fronts.[6]

He went on to accuse the Left wing of never having understood this He called for a dialogue on the questions this combination of nationalism and socialism in Scotland would raise within the SLP.

But such cool attempts to reason together were uncommon. More indicative of the mood within the SLP was this warning, sent to all Edinburgh members on November 3rd (the Wednesday after the Stirling Congress):

WARNING AGAINST IMITATIONS . . .

An advertisement for an "SLP Public Meeting" today (Thursday) has appeared in the press. This is NOT, repeat NOT a genuine meeting of

6. Nairn, Tom, *The National Question.*

the Scottish Labour Party, but a function set up by members of the Trotskyite minority recently removed from the party. You have been warned.[7]

It seems that someone realised that Sillars' reassuring words in a cyclostyled letter to his members of November 1st, "The new NEC will do everything possible to encourage a free flow of ideas and dialogue", was just so much window dressing. On the contrary, those who were going to stay in would have to recognise the boss; preferably they should be seen to do so.

It is conceivable that if the SLP had been built of the kind of robots who would follow "the working class way" and "display unquestioning loyalty to every move the leadership made" — if there are such people — this membership would have stayed loyal. But there were few such members.

In the ensuing months whole branches dropped off. The Edinburgh branches — who on the eve of the Stirling Congress had nearly 1/9th of the membership — have disappeared. The Glasgow and Dundee branches have been reorganised so that there is one branch in each city; both have trouble functioning. Of the forty-one branches which existed in October 1976, seventeen: Airdrie, Dundee Central, Dundee Whitfield, Bonnybridge, Cumbernauld, Dunfermline, Edinburgh South, Edinburgh North-Central, Glasgow Kelvin, Glasgow Pollok, Hamilton, Irvine, Leven, St Andrews, St Andrews University, Stirling and Stirling University — have ceased to function. The remnants of some of these branches have been reorganised into other branches, and there have been some new branches formed such as one in Dalkeith and another in London (both were notified to the February 6th NEC meeting). Nevertheless, the deceased branches had 333 votes (37% of the total) at the Stirling Congress. As in any other party, there are a number of active branches and a number of paper branches. One test of an active branch is the submission of resolutions or nominations to the Party Annual Congress. Only sixteen branches submitted nominations, emergency resolutions or amendments to the Constitution to the 1977 Congress. They were Aberdeen, Aberdeen University, Ayr, Cumnock, Cumnock Landward, Dundee Central, Dundee Whitfield (despite these last two meeting together as a single branch), Fife, Glasgow West, Glasgow University, Larbert, Law, Moray, Paisley

7. Anonymous.
8. *List of Nominations for the National Executive Committee* (Ayr, Congress '77). *List of Amendments to Resolution* (Ayr, Congress '77); *Emergency Resolutions* (Ayr, Congress '77); *List of Nominees for Party Officers* (Ayr, Congress '77).

and Patna.[8] Of these, five are in Ayrshire and of the branches outside Ayrshire only Aberdeen seems to have any vitality. Of the five officers and fifteen NEC members elected at Stirling, four (Danus Skene — Executive Vice-Chairman — and Jimmy Allardice, Roddy McKenzie and Bob Tait) were from Aberdeen. McKenzie did not seek re-election in 1977. The others were returned with two more Aberdonians, Lindsay Paterson and Isobel Murray.

The Party's money problems could no longer be hidden once the Stirling Congress was over. The delegates to the Congress had been presented with a financial report which showed total income as £5,898.65 and total expenditure as £5,795.43 and that the Party had a balance of £103.22.[9] At the first NEC meeting, two weeks after the Congress, the new Treasurer, Tom Yates, revealed that, in fact, the Party had a deficit of £1,000 and had a loan of £250 in addition. Moreover, the Party had a monthly shortfall of at least £130 which resulted in an ever-increasing deficit. Equally depressing was his revelation that only £500 had been raised of the needed £9,000 for the Parliamentary election fund.[10] He proposed a financial appeal, as well as other measures to cure the problem. At the following NEC meeting the Treasurer reported that a mere £80 had been raised from this appeal. Money remained a large problem.[11]

The recall Congress had to be postponed from December to January because Alex Neil was unable to book a hall in time for December.[12] When it did meet it was a tame and frightened affair; the press was allowed in but not visitors; the only opposition to the platform's policies came from NEC member Sheila Gilmore who protested — in vain — at the consumerism of "Jobs and Industry". Secretary Alex Neil's *Report* of the two Congresses omitted to mention the Leith suspension, any of the emergency resolutions, or the expulsions. It also omitted the phrase "as a first step towards this" from the Glasgow University Foreign Policy Resolution (see above Chapter VI part II). Having failed to control their Congress the leaders attempted to falsify history.

Slowly life seemed to be disappearing from the Party. A weekend school for prospective candidates and their agents originally scheduled for the 26th and 27th of February was not held because of insufficient registrations.[13] The March meeting of the National

9. The Scottish Labour Party; *Financial Report January-September 1977* p. 1.
10. *Minute of November 13th NEC* p. 2.
11. *Minute of December 12th NEC* p. 2.
12. Letter from Alex Neil to NEC members of 30th November 1976.
13. *Minute of March 6th NEC* p. 1. and *Report of the First Annual Congress* Stirling-October 1976, Glasgow January 1977.

Council (at which each branch is entitled to two delegates) was held in Perth. About fifty members attended. At the June meeting in Dundee there were a bare twenty. The NEC operated on much the same basis as the NOC before it, save that it spent much of its time in the months before the summer of 1977 clearing up the mess created at Stirling. One such mess was a collection for the Scottish Chilean Defence Committee. A speaker from one of the many Chilean campaigns had been heard at the Stirling Congress and a collection was taken for his group at the end of his speech. After the speech the party had decided to affiliate to the Chilean campaign (the *Report* of the Congress omitted any mention of this incident too). The Minute of the February meeting records, laconically, that more care would have to be taken in the future as there had been an embarrassing dispute over what happened to the money.[14] But perhaps the most obvious way in which the NEC was treated like the NOC before it concerned publicity. NEC meetings were treated as occasions for the publication of press statements; not as decision-making meetings.

A frank justification of this practice was contained in an *Interim Report on Propaganda and Publicity* which was written on December 9th 1976 and distributed to the NEC. It stated:

> It is imperative that the party and the NEC, while consulting with its MPs at every opportunity consistent with the reality of their "independent" status, per se, as MPs for South Ayrshire and Paisley, reposes maximum confidence in the MPs faithfully to outline SLP policy where this had been formulated, and where it has not, to interpret it acceptably (even if this is done on a personalised basis) along with the line which it seems reasonable to assume the SLP will develop its stance. Clearly scope exists for misjudgment on occasion, but there has to be mutual respect and trust between the SLP and its MPs, otherwise it will become virtually impossible for the party to maintain a steady flow of "propaganda" via the media which instead will need to concentrate attention on the MPs as individual Members rather than party associates.[15]

In other words, 'be still and let the MPs speak your name — that way your name will be spread abroad'. This is very much what the party put into practice when it produced its draft Devolution Bill. On Thursday March 3rd, Sillars had announced that the SLP was to publish its alternative Devolution Bill in the following week. At the

14. *Minute of February 5th NOC* p. 1.
15. Brown, Bob and Frame, Jim *The Scottish Labour party: Interim Report to the NEC on Propaganda and Publicity* December 9th 1976 (grammar and syntax as in the original).

NEC meeting of March 6th this was the last item of business. When it was raised, Sheila Gilmore asked if the NEC was to be given the opportunity to discuss the Bill. She objected to the public announcement which had pre-empted any possibility that the NEC or the NC (which met immediately after the NEC) might be able to decide whether it was desirable to have a draft Bill — let alone what would be in one. Sillars defended his decision to announce the Bill as a matter of urgency which had to be left to the MPs. The NEC was not asked whether it wanted to have this Bill in the name of the party. The Minute of the NEC simply states "Jim Sillars gave a report on the reasons behind this Bill".[16]

Of course, all parties have 'timing' problems of this kind. If an MP or party leader is to make any press impact he has to respond to events quickly in order to meet press interest. The fact that the MPs are called upon to make statements on various subjects at short notice — and that they, and not the NEC, are asked — is one of the sources of their power over their NECs. This is true of the large parties as well as of the SLP, but it was a real problem for the SLP because it had attracted idealists who believed that the new party would be something different — something genuinely democratic. The tension between consulting one's party and making newsworthy statements was particularly severe in the case of the SLP, because the Party was aware that its strength lay in its ability to use the press successfully. As the *Interim Report* noted:

> The propaganda activities and opportunities open to the SLP have to be at all times realistically assessed in relation to the financial and manpower resources at the party's command which place severe limitations on what can be accomplished. Nevertheless, much is possible provided determination and skill is applied to the situation generally and the opportunities represented by the Media (both Press and Broadcasting) continue to be extensively exploited in the manner which is by now well established and which has already served the party magnificently.[17]

And yet even as this statement was made that magnificent service was becoming a thing of the past. Their last great burst of news coverage occurred during the Stirling Congress. On the Sunday, the expulsions were the first item of BBC news broadcasts all day. After that when news or current affairs programmes had spokesmen from the parties on some event, the SLP was no longer normally included. The NEC Minute of the December 12th meeting recorded that the

16. *Minute of March 6th NEC* and Interview with Sheila Gilmore.
17. Brown, Bob and Frame, Jim *Op. Cit.* p. 1.

Daily Record had refused to take an advertisement from the SLP.[18] Sadly, one of the rare occasions after the Congress when the party received publicity was on December 22nd when they reported a burglary from their offices.

One possible measure of the SLP's news value is Stewart MacLachlan's weekly column in the *Daily Record* each Friday. MacLachlan's column normally carries several stories. As the following table shows, in the early months of the SLP it was frequently mentioned. But it began to drop out of the news after the Darnley by-election (1st June) and nearly disappeared after the Stirling Congress:

Date	Coverage	Date	Coverage
19.12.75	Story	7.5.76	no column
26.12.75	no column	14.5.76	Story
2.1.76	no paper	21.5.76	no column
9.1.76	no mention	28.5.76	no column
16.1.76	Story	4.6.76	Story
23.1.76	Story	11.6.76	no mention
30.1.76	Story	18-25.6.76	Column written by T. Taylor
6.2.76	Story	2.7.76	no column
13.2.76	Reference	9.7.76	Story
20.2.76	Story	16.7.76	no mention
27.2.76	Reference	23.7.76	no mention
5.3.76	Story	30.7.76	no mention
12.3.76	Story	6.8.76	no mention
19.3.76	Reference	13.8.76 to	no
26.3.76	no column	8.10.76	column
2.4.76	no mention	15.10.76	no mention
9.4.76	no column	22.10.76	no mention
16.4.76	Reference	29.10.76	Story
23.4.76	no column	November	one reference
30.4.76	Story	December	no mention [19]

After Stirling the only angle the press could find space for was 'the break up of the SLP' story. For instance, Stewart MacLachlan's story for April 1st 1977 read:

> Is the breakaway Scottish Labour Party about to fade away from the Scottish political scene after just over a year's existence?
> It would appear to be the case. For I understand that Jim Sillars, the SLP's founder and MP for South Ayrshire plans to quit. . . If

18. *Minute of December 12th* NEC p. 1.
19. MacLachlan, S. "From the Inside" *Daily Record* 19th December 1975- December 1976.

Jim Sillars goes — and I am told this is very much on the cards — the SLP will lose its parliamentary leadership.[20]

This same column also indicated that John Robertson was unlikely to stand again for Parliament. Robertson announced that decision in October 1977.

Another measure of the news-value of a party is its treatment by the broadcasting authorities. The BBC and the commercial radio and television stations are required by law to be 'balanced, fair and objective'. This requirement is difficult to translate into actual practice. No radio or television station asks the Co-operative or the Communist Party for their reactions to the defeat of specific Bills; nor do they send camera teams to those parties' Annual Conferences. Thus it is interesting that the BBC did not feel it necessary to have the SLP point of view represented on the air during its discussions of the government's loss of the 'guillotine' on the Scotland and Wales (Devolution) Bill. Neither did it have a representative of the SLP — or the Communist or Co-operative Parties for that matter — on its District Election (May 1977) analysis programmes. On the other hand it did send a team to the SLP's second Congress at Ayr in October 1977 from which Chris Baur could be seen giving a Congress Report each night.

Things might have gone differently for the Party had there been a General Election before, or even immediately after, the Stirling Congress. An election would have rallied the membership. It would have strengthened the hand of the Leaders. Victory, even if only in South Ayrshire, would have established the party as nothing else could. It is clear from the NOC's Minutes that Sillars expected a General Election in the Spring or Summer of 1976. Had he retained South Ayrshire then, while Labour lost a dozen or so seats to the SNP, his position would have been immensely improved. Deprived of a General Election the party had to make do with the May 1977 District (local government) elections.

The Official Party had thirty-five candidates. The Scottish Socialist League contested a dozen seats. A renegade group in Douglas (Dundee) which had unsuccessfully applied for affiliation to the SLP in May 1976 also put up three candidates in the name of the SLP. The Official Party won three seats.

They retained the Clydebank seat of Whitecrook where the sitting SNP Councillor Ian Smith had joined the SLP shortly after its

20. MacLachlan, "Inside Politics" *Daily Record* 1 April, 1977 p. 3.

formation. In South Ayrshire the party won two seats: Old Cumnock Parish and Patna. In these three seats the party faced an SNP opponent only in Patna. The main variable in the SLP performance seems to have been whether or not the SNP put up a candidate. In the seventeen seats which both the SLP and the SNP contested, the SLP's average vote was 12.6%. In the nineteen seats where the SLP did not face an SNP opponent its average vote was 26.8% (these two sets of contests are not strictly comparable since there were an average of 3.9 candidates in the seats both SNP and SLP contested, but only 3.0 in the seats where the SLP did not face SNP competition). Another important variable was place. The SLP performed better in the Ayrshire Districts (Cunningham; Kilmarnock and Loudon; Kyle and Carrick; and Cumnock and Doon Valley) than elsewhere. In Ayrshire Districts it won 24.9% of the vote; elsewhere 17.2% of the vote. Indeed, within Ayrshire it performed consistently well in the areas where it had the largest branches: in Kyle and Carrick and in Cumnock and Doon Valley.[21] As the District boundaries do not correspond directly with the boundaries of Parliamentary Constituencies it is difficult from these results to predict how the party might perform at a future General Election. In addition, at an election the party would also face SNP opposition everywhere. Nevertheless, it looks as if the SLP would do best to challenge several Ayrshire seats. *Forward Scotland* characterised the SLP's performance in the May District Elections as a "Brave Show".[22] It was just that.

But the biggest disappointment for the SLP — especially after Stirling — was their irrelevance to the devolution debate in the House of Commons. Sillars and Robertson both spoke freely during the debate especially when the House debated the Second Reading of the Bill. In addition they tabled twenty-eight amendments to the Bill. After the government lost the vote on the 'guillotine' the Leader of the House — Michael Foot — had talks with all the parties about what to do. Sillars and Robertson took this opportunity to table a draft Bill in the name of the SLP which Litster Gardiner had drawn up. But it made little difference. The government eventually re-introduced a slightly amended Bill which made small concessions to the Liberals and the Ulster Unionists — but none to the SLP. The party had little role in Westminster. Sillars acknowledged this when

21. See Appendix C.
22. Anonymous, "A Brave Show at the Polls" *Forward Scotland* Vol. 1 No. 4 July 1977.

he announced in October 1977 that he would not stand for Parliament again if the government created the Scottish Assembly before the next General Election. Thus partly through ill luck, and partly through its own inability to find a positive role for itself, the SLP continued its sleepwalk begun at Stirling in October 1976 for the following year. It retained life but did not regain consciousness and showed signs of drifting lower as time went on.

Chapter VIII:

The Import of the SLP

The SLP was intended to fill a gap in Scottish politics between the National Party and the Labour Party. It was to appeal to those who would follow a banner on which both 'Scotland' and 'Socialism' were emblazoned. It was created out of the conviction that some kind of Scottish Labour Party was inevitable and the hope that December 1975, in the wake of the SNP's discredit over EEC membership and the Labour Party's discredit over its White paper on devolution — was the right time to move. The decision to create this Scottish Labour Party in December 1975, rather than wait for the creation of an Assembly was always a gamble. The move might prove premature if the Government failed to deliver devolution and it might, on the other hand, be too late if the SNP had already rallied all the Scottish Socialist support that could be drawn out of the Labour Party. The founders of the SLP were never so sure about the rightness of their timing as they were about the necessity for their party to be created at some time. Given that the first months of the party were so frenzied and that the SLP is now so obviously in retreat, it is tempting for people to turn around and blame it all on Jim Sillars. It will be said that he spoiled a great opportunity by bad timing. Is this really fair?

One of the first things which happened after the SLP was created was that the two parties between whom it was supposed to live, moved to squeeze it out. Both the Labour and National parties have moved to more decisive positions on the national question since January 1976. The Labour Party's Scottish Council urged its Scottish Conference in March 1976 to adopt a stronger pro-devolution stance. Conference complied. This, as Sillars noted at his

133

party's Conference at Middleton Hall, was a move in the SLP's direction. But it was a move which narrowed the ground on which the SLP could stand. For a young party supposedly set up on ideological (as opposed to interest) grounds this was a dangerous loss. The National Party also shifted to a more radical stand. At its Annual Conference in May 1977 the SNP abandoned its commitment to devolution as a step to independence. It would fight the next election on a promise of independence. Thus both Labour and the National Party have moved to distinctive stands on devolution, each being more radical than previously.

The SLP's response to this has been increasingly to emphasise the sense in which its "Scotland in Europe" formula requires an independent Scotland. It has not actually changed its formula, but changed the emphasis it puts on this part of it. It is impossible to say definitely whether the entry of the SLP onto the scene was the cause of the other parties' shifts. It is at least plausible that the momentum of the move to devolution which was so important to the creation of the SLP also moved the Labour and National Parties' policies. All the opinion polls published during the SLP's lifetime have shown a constant 60% of Scots in favour of a degree of devolution and 20% in favour of outright independence. This was motive enough to make the existing parties want to portray themselves as convincingly as possible as being 'for Scotland'. Nevertheless, it is impossible to escape the impression that the creation of the SLP, and the favourable publicity which it attracted, was a great shock to the Labour party and was an additional factor in its calculations.

But the fight which, more than anything else, shaped the SLP and determined its history had nothing whatever to do with either devolution or the National or Labour Parties. It was the fight to expel IMG and the 'trouble-makers'. This struggle was the major factor in the SLP's history from the beginning to its climactic Congress at Stirling. The anxiety of the leaders over any taint of Trotskyism was an important reason for their tepid commitment to Socialist schemes. They feared that the adoption of any vaguely 'red' proposal would reinforce the impression that Trotskyists were in — perhaps even create the impression that Trotskyists controlled — the party. Certainly they were right to fear that any extra-electoral socialism, such as aiding the strikers in Cumbernauld, might have attracted more Trotskyists into the party.

But the SLP reacted too sharply and in the process alienated first the Glasgow members and eventually much of the party. At no one time did the IMG have more than two dozen active members in the SLP. They were concentrated in only three areas, Leith (where they certainly should have been controllable), Glasgow (where the branch could easily have controlled them had it not been for the Balkanising policy of the NOC) and Aberdeen (where they were in fact controlled). Against this the NOC had the undivided support of the ex-IMG members of the SWRP who were only too willing to help by revealing the tactics and strategy of the IMG and by identifying IMG members. The NOC might also have realised that the IMG's public commitment to their new party had put the IMG in a weak and exposed position. They had joined a Social Democratic electoral party and would be ridiculed by other Trotskyists — for example the more numerous members of the Socialist Workers Party — if they could not produce results. They would also have been in a weak position if the leadership had ever threatened them privately with expulsion. This is borne out by IMG's action over the Kelvin Resolution. When faced with expulsion they retreated from every position.

Were the IMG ever a threat to the SLP? The image the leaders used constantly to justify their action after Stirling was that of a weed that would strangle a young tree. Their new party was, they thought, too weak and too young to stand the presence of the IMG. Hence the imperative to cut the IMG down. There were a good many members of the SLP, including some who left after Stirling, who agreed with their views. The fact is that the IMG has a terrible reputation on the Left. Its machinations may have done it — and the revolution — little good, but they have convinced many people that IMG is a curse which ruins everything it touches. On the other hand, some SLP members who are still active and were in branches which had IMG members have told me that they don't know what the fuss was about. They had no real problem.

The SLP leaders could not know it, but the IMG had decided to pull out of their organisation and get involved in other 'class-struggle' activities even before the October Congress. In their June document Comrades Ure and Coltrane actually mentioned this decision and urged that the date be brought forward.[1] But even though the NOC was not aware of this decision — which made the whole struggle at Stirling completely unnecessary — they might have tried to turn the IMG entry to advantage by beating them politically rather than throwing them out so violently. This could have been done in two different ways (and nearly was even without being

1. Ure and Coltrane Op. Cit.

135

intended). The first was simply to outnumber the IMG. In a democratic organisation twenty-four members are no match for eight hundred and sixty. The other way to defeat the IMG politically would have been to avoid all extra-electoral activity until the IMG departed and defeat any obviously IMG inspired resolutions at Congress. There were non-IMG left wing resolutions which the leadership could have backed, such as the resolutions from Stirling and Cumnock on the nationalisation of the banks, which would have shown the non-IMG left that the leaders were not mindless red-bashers. This path was not followed. As a consequence the IMG presence became an irritation which grew out of all proportion.

The difficulties the party had with its IMG members does, however, throw into dramatic relief the real cost which IMG is to the Left. A fair number of the people in what Comrade MacPherson called the 'atomised left' are ex-IMG members; others are former members of other revolutionary organisations. These former Trotskyists are very wary of their old Comrades. Many of them left because they became disenchanted with the endless wranglings of the Trotskyist form of democracy. The fact that IMG and the other Trotskyist groups tend to adopt every conceivable left wing cause has the effect of scaring other people off these causes. My impression is that as a result of their experience in the SLP, many of its members will join (in some cases rejoin) the Labour Party, for it alone is big enough to smother Trotskyist members. The leaders of Dundee branch of the SLP decided to do this en masse in November 1977. In this way Trotskyist activity helps to build the Labour Party. In the short run, at any rate, the major effect of the SLP — which was supposed to be a middle way between the SNP and the Labour Party — has been to strengthen both the Nationalists and Labour by showing people in both of these parties how difficult it is to follow the middle road.

The import of the SLP extends, however, far beyond its relations with the IMG. The history of the Party raises some important questions about the press and its relationship to political parties. There was nothing exceptional in the fact that many journalists worked for the SLP. After all, most of them had been working within the Labour Party for years before they even conceived of the SLP. What was exceptional was the degree of their involvement in the party and the success of their efforts to gain favourable publicity for it. It is too much to say that the SLP was a press plot or even that its creation was a press plot. But it cannot be denied that without press encouragement the SLP would never have been created in the form it was, when it was, by the people who created it. That journalists were prominent in the party cannot be disputed; its first Chairman and current Press Officer, Bob Brown, was a journalist turned Information Officer; two other members of its original organising Committee of seven, Jim Fyfe and Jimmy Frame, were also journalists and they were later joined by Neal Ascherson. A number of other journalists while not so prominent in the party's organisation, were active in it. Some of them, while active in the Party, reported the news in their papers. This relationship between the new party and the press suggests a number of questions which need to be considered separately.

There is, first of all, the question of bias. A number of recent theoretical and empirical studies have emphasised the various ways bias is "built into" the collection and dissemination of news.[2] My concern here, however, is with something much more immediate; journalists as observers and participants in the same events. Ideologies conflict on this question. There is firstly, a tradition of neutrality amongst journalists. This is perhaps the dominant ideology amongst Scottish political journalists at the present. On the other hand there is also a tradition of committed (a more acceptable word than 'biased') journalism on the Continent and 'advocacy journalism' in the United States. The existence of the SLP's non-card carrying members in the Press is an indication that the two ideologies were at work and were conflicting with one another. Why should people at once support at party, give it money and encouragement, and yet not carry its card unless they feared there was something improper about commitment?

These non-card carrying members were caught in an ideological trap. It is a trap which is peculiarly strong in journalism. The rules about the political involvement of civil servants and academics — two other professions which are expected to profess neutrality — are fairly well worked out and agreed. Civil Servants may be members of political parties, but may not hold office or take a public role in the activities of their parties. Academics, on the other hand, are not barred from political activity. Some are councillors, many are prominent activists in the various parties. I, myself, am Chairman of a Constituency Labour Party. Journalists do not have such clearly demarcated rules to guide them.

Most newspapers purport to be more than mouthpieces for

2. See, for example, Tom Burns *The BBC: A Public Institution in a Private World* and Glasgow University Media Group *Bad News*.

particular parties or interests, paying at least some attention to the familiar dictum, originally enunciated by C. P. Scott, "Comment is free, but facts are sacred". The maintenance of this distinction, no simple task, is generally held to be of value to the public. It can also be useful to the journalist who is under pressure from an editor or politician. Yet the requirement to be neutral can be a curb on a reporter. All men have values and political reporters often feel strongly about political events. The journalists who played such a vital role in creating and running the SLP were showing their willingness to break out of the protective shell of neutrality.

Time and again in my interviews with the members of the mini-cadre, I was struck by their enraged frustration with the constraints imposed on them both by their professional ideology and by the Labour Party. The one insisted that they had no political rights. The other refused to heed their private advice. The SLP was their answer when both became intolerable. As political observers within the Labour Party they had been in effect political voyeurs. They had spent years watching other people's miserable attempts to consummate their power lust, and were — as the price of being able to watch —forbidden to act themselves. Come the Labour Party's fumblings over devolution and they could stand it no more.

But the old ideology is far from dead. For every journalist who joined the SLP and worked for it — openly or not — there was another who felt, often quite strongly, that his colleagues had let the profession down. Furthermore the abandonment of the ideology of neutrality for the ideology of commitment has consequences which those who made the jump seem not yet willing to face. People who are committed to a cause have no right to hide that commitment from their audience.

The creation of the SLP came, as I have pointed out, at a time when the Scottish political Press was expanding. There were more journalists around who regularly reported on political events in Scotland. This expansion meant that any Scottish political news could expect more coverage than it would have received in the previous generation. The new expansion and self-confidence which came with it found expression in various ways; the SLP was not its only product. Another product of it was APCIS: the Association of Political Correspondents in Scotland. This association (with its singularly awkward acronym) was set up in the late Spring of 1976. Its purpose is to care for the interests of the political correspondents. It was formed when the Scottish Office and the newspaper publishers were meeting to decide on the arrangements for reporting the activities of the new Assembly. The first purpose of APCIS was to ensure that its twenty odd members had a say in these arrangements. They were particularly concerned to ensure that the establishment of the Assembly did not lead to the re-creation in Edinburgh of the Lobby system which operates in Westminster. This — admirable — intention was, like their role in the SLP, an active intervention in politics. It is quite a different matter, from bias, and it is quite inconceivable that it would have happened without the increase in the numbers of political correspondents.

Yet it can be doubted whether the heavy involvement of journalists in the SLP was to the party's advantage. The party as we have seen, concentrated its energies on the publicly visible facets of politics — the parts journalists see — it was built around an attractive quotable MP, held press conferences on every possible occasion, based its policy on a few clever phrases — 'Scotland in Europe' for example — published policy statements without taking proper time to consider them, made wildly exaggerated claims of membership, held a large public Congress which was dressed up to resemble other parties' Conferences, and threw out the Trotskyists in public. It ignored the private aspects of politics. Its founders never came to grips with the party's finances — indeed, they launched it with hardly a thought about money; they turned their backs on the superb South Ayrshire Constituency Labour Party; they never seriously courted the unions; they made little attempt to consult or work with their activists — there wasn't even so much as a good journal with a Letters column for the exchange of ideas; they had only the haziest and ill-conceived ideas about the social basis of their party. The SLP became a hectic campaign. It made a lot of noise.

Furthermore, the collapse of the publicity for the new party in the summer of 1976 points to the limitations of journalists as a base of political support. The 'James Alexander' articles, the *Scotsman's* encouragment for the party, the blaze of favourable publicity which greeted its creation, the useful support from Stewart MacLachlan, are all of a piece. And they all stopped short a bare six months after the SLP was created. This will hardly do as a basis for a political party. Parties must survive for years between elections, and sometimes from lost election to lost election, when they have no news value whatever. Six months is a short time in politics.

The collapse of press interest in the SLP is a sign that the sympathy of journalists without the whole-hearted support of their editors and beyond them, their publishers, is a diminishing asset. After a while, most stories grow cold. People get bored. This is true of the whole devolution story. It was a kind of wave which swept through Scottish political life in the 1970's and which reached a peak at the end of 1975. The SLP was the crest of this particular wave and when the wave subsided shortly after the SLP's creation the press interest in the party subsided too (it may of course rise again). If the Scottish political press cannot sustain interest in a story like devolution in which it has a direct and undeniable stake and to which the Scottish newspapers have a clear and unequivocable commitment, could it really be expected to sustain publicity for a political party in which most had no such investment?

A comparison of the position of the SLP and SNP in this regard makes the point much clearer. The Press have been attracted to the SNP three times in the party's history. The first was shortly after the party was formed. It was at this time that Lord Beaverbrook was trying to make a go of the Scottish edition of his *Daily Express*.[3] John MacCormick records in his autobiographical account of the early days of the SNP (or National Party as it then was) that Beaverbrook was having trouble establishing his paper and realised he needed a Scottish angle. Beaverbrook sought out MacCormick and asked his advice. MacCormick told him to stop advertising London cinemas in his paper, call it the *Scottish Daily Express* and back the National Party. Beaverbrook, a Canadian of Scottish extraction, took the advice. His paper was then in competition with the *Daily Record* for Scottish readers. The Beaverbrook paper backed the National Party candidate in Edinburgh East in the 1931 General Election. MacCormick records that in the 1931 General Election "so far as the columns of the *Express* were concerned he (the SNP candidate, T. T. Alexander) was regarded as practically the only candidate in Scotland".[4] David Anderson, editor of the *Daily Record* was no less committed but believed that middle-class Scots (the audience he wanted) would be repelled by the National Party.[5] In 1931 as today political allegiances and alignments were changing. But soon after 1931 the two-party system reasserted itself and both papers lost interest in the SNP.

When the young John MacCormick was so boldly telling the Press

3. This account of the relationships between MacCormick and the Press comes from MacCormick's book *A Flag in the Wind: The Story of the National Movement in Scotland* (London, 1955) pp 38 *et seq* pp 50-65
4. MacCormick, J. *Op. Cit.*, p. 50.
5. MacCormick, J. *Op. Cit.*, p. 72.

Lord how to run his papers, Beaverbrook gave MacCormick some advice too; spend your time building your machine; work up through local government, put all your efforts into one town, capture control of it, and everyone will sit up and take notice. MacCormick knew that his party wasn't up to this effort. When Beaverbrook realised that his advice was not being taken he withdrew his support. The next time the press took up the SNP, at the time of the Hamilton by-election in 1966, that had changed.[6] By then the SNP had about two hundred active local branches in most areas of Scotland. This time the Press was backing a party which could stand on its own and survive without press interest — much though the attention was welcome. In fact, the SNP did survive the loss of press interest which occurred in 1969 (after the May local elections) and continued until the Dundee by-election in 1972.

The contrast then, between press interest in the SNP and the SLP is very strong. The SNP attracted support, in the first instance, from a Press Lord, not journalists. He was capable of using his paper to suit his political whim and did use it freely in the cause of the National Party as well as for his other enthusiasms such as 'Empire Free Trade'. The subsequent periods of press interest in the SNP came at a time when the party had other strengths. The SNP could carry on when it lost favour in 1969, and though there was ill feeling and some bitterness about the loss, it was not fatal. The SLP, on the other hand, was supported by journalists. Unlike Lord Beaverbrook, they did not have a free hand. Moreover, the new party was so dependent on publicity to maintain momentum and bring in new members that when the flow of favourable publicity ceased in the summer of 1976 it was a very damaging blow.

III

A political party which is to have the faintest chance of surviving for more than a year or two needs to have and to understand its social base. It is almost incredible that this point should have to be made against a Socialist party in twentieth century Britain. Sillars and his mini-cadre would seem to have completely misunderstood the society to which they would appeal for support.

They mistook South Ayrshire for Scotland. Before he set up his own party, Sillars was adored by his constituents. He had an intense following in the Doon Valley. The Doon Valley is the epitome of the old Scotland. It is an area of small towns and mining villages. It also,

6. Interviews with Stephen Maxwell and Jack Brand.

unfortunately, has a 40% male unemployment rate. It is intensely proud of its own. It has a very strong NUM and is the heart of the South Ayrshire Constituency Labour Party. When Sillars looked for unquestioning loyalty from his SLP members he was,in effect, hoping they would give him the kind of loyalty he expected from the people of the Doon Valley.

There were a number of flaws in this picture. For one thing the kind of loyalty Sillars knew in South Ayrshire is extended only to those who return it. Sillars' break from the Labour Party was immediately castigated by the NUM as betrayal. The January 1976 issue of the Scottish NUM's journal *Scottish Miner* reported the decision of the Union's Executive on December 22nd (1975) to "regret" the decision to establish the SLP. "United we stand, divided we fall", was the lesson, and Sillars was a divider. Sillars further compounded his sin by failing actively to support the miners at the Cairnhill Pit in his constituency when the NCB moved to close it. The Communist Party, which has a presence in the Doon Valley, is a strong supporter of united action by the working class — which means it supports Labour Governments. The Communist and Labour Parties in Ayrshire will not lightly forgive Sillars' vote with the Conservatives in the March 1977 motion of 'no confidence' in the Labour Government. The nail was further driven home on that occasion by the fact that the government had a 'Coal Bill' before the House of Commons. This Bill promised large investments in the South Ayrshire mines. Defeat for the Government would have meant the loss of this Bill. The loyalty to Sillars in South Ayrshire must be sorely tried. Nonetheless, South Ayrshire was one social base of the SLP.[7]

But the most fundamental flaw in the SLP's social analysis was its failure to realise that Scotland was changing rapidly. 'Jobs and Industry' showed this. It lamented particularly the loss of jobs in manufacturing industries and their replacement with a smaller number of jobs in public administration and service industries. This loss is indeed the root of many of Scotland's social problems and the

7. A recent study by an Aberdeen University student suggests that Sillars was never really accepted by the South Ayrshire Miners even before his break because their candidate failed to get the Labour nomination in 1970. This study, compiled in August/September 1976, also shows that only 3% of the miners interviewed would have voted for him if there had been an election the next day (71% said Labour: 3% said SNP) but 43% of the sample expected Sillars to hold his seat at the next election. See Reilly, Michael *Opinions and Attitudes of Some Ayrshire Miners.* (Typescript available from the Aberdeen University Politics Dept.) pp. 1-4; 10-12

K

net loss of jobs in certainly a source for regret. But the notion that Scotland can expect to attract more manufacturing industry jobs and that these jobs are somehow superior to other jobs is unconvincing. An industrial Scotland dominated by extractive and heavy industry as it was in the period between 1880 and 1920, and, though to a lesser extent, up to about 1960, has passed away. There are fewer and fewer such jobs to be had. Scotland, like the rest of the industrialised world, will have to adapt. The impressive thing about Scotland, since the 1960 census was taken, is that — partly as a result of government regional policy — it has attracted new jobs in new industries. A new Scotland of public administrators, teachers and privately owned light industries is emerging. This new Scotland ought to be the social basis of any new party. Certainly the SNP has learned this lesson and has performed particularly well in the areas where this new Scotland lives: paradigmatically it has done well in the New Towns.

Sillars' party paid a price for its failure to perceive this and for its failure to appreciate that its activists came, largely, despite the party's appeal to the old Scotland, from radicalised sections of the new Scotland. Carol Craig, an Edinburgh post-graduate student and Secretary of the Edinburgh North/Central branch of the SLP summarised this incongruity when she said, "Sillars' problem was that he wanted my father — who's a railwayman — to join; what he got was me".[8] Sillars had in fact succeeded in gathering together a substantial number of energetic, intelligent, hard-working, idealistic young people from a large number of different Scottish towns and cities. Like CND the party brought together people who felt strongly about an idea — in this case, about Scottish Socialism — and who wanted to campaign for their idea. Many of them had actually been in CND. These people had quite different interests and talents from those who normally dominate political parties. They lacked the patience of the party worthies who will sit in the cold committee rooms of their traditional parties just keeping the local machine in existence, knowing that it is enough simply to be present when the next General Election occurs. They lacked people who would go from doorstep to doorstep night after night — Sillars berated his Edinburgh members for just this failure — checking out the party vote, talking, as Sillars put it, to "real people". But perhaps this did not matter, that is not the kind of party they were. And it is doubtful if any new party will be like that again. The supply of political worthies is drying up as the traditional parties are finding to

8. Interview with Carol Craig.

143

their cost. Christopher Harvie has said that the SLP was an officer corps in search of an army. The comment is unkind, but not without point. These SLP members were writers of pamphlets, signers of petitions, framers of resolutions: not party loyalists. In them Sillars and Neil had the basis of an impressive campaigning party. This was the second social base of the new party.

If nothing else, the SLP has demonstrated that Scotland possesses a goodly amount of unused political energy. It is sometimes claimed that Scotland does not produce a very impressive group of MPs or councillors. The history of the SLP suggests that, in our time at least, this failure may have something to do with the unattractiveness of the existing political parties as vehicles for action, to a fair section of the Scotland's potential activists.

IV

But if the SLP's members were an officer corps without an army they had a general — a leader who would make sense of the whole project: Sillars. His position in the SLP was very similar to that of an American presidential candidate. Without him the campaign would be meaningless. His often reiterated resignation threats served to remind the party who was boss. This SLP is no democracy. And here is the fundamental contradiction in its make-up. I have been struck by the deeply ingrained belief in democracy and strong dislike of authority in a large number of the SLP's activists. These beliefs made it extremely difficult for the SLP, organised as it was around its charismatic leader, to keep together. The brutality of the Stirling Congress simply hastened a disenchantment which would have been difficult to avoid in any case. The effect of the psycho-drama at Stirling has been to focus attention on Sillars and Neil and distract attention from more fundamental problems. As Tom Nairn has suggested, it takes someone of Sillars' bravery and willpower to break away from an existing party and set up a new one.[9] It is difficult to see how a new party which is to make any impact can be created except by the action of men as prominent as Sillars. After all, the SLP — with all its difficulties — is a vastly more significant enterprise than the SWRP was, or ever could have been. Yet, by the same token, men of Sillars' forcefulness are not suited to running democratic organisations, and only democratic organisations are likely to sustain the support of any large number of intelligent

9. Nairn T. "The SLP: Report on the First Year of a New Party" *Planet* 38/39 May 1977 pp. 14-17.

activists. This is a real dilemma. The history of the British Left in the twentieth century is littered with the corpses of unsuccessful breakaway parties.

There is a further, and for the Left, a more worrying problem; is there any longer sufficient popular support for a new Socialist party? It was noticeable that both the Labour and the National parties moved to more radical stands on the Scottish question after the creation of the SLP. But neither moved to take up more radical Socialist positions. Is this not because they sense that there is no significant popular demand for a more left-wing party amongst the electors? Putting together a party with two MPs, a handful of councillors and nine hundred or so activists in a year is one thing — but winning Parliamentary or Assembly (or EEC) elections might be quite another thing. There is now substantial survey evidence suggesting that the Labour Party is a good few degrees to the left of its electorate on many social issues. Richard Rose has shown that the social attitudes of Labour's voters coincide more closely with those of Conservative MPs than with those of Labour MPs.[10] Ivor Crewe has shown that even those voters who strongly support Labour do not agree with the party's socialist policies. And there are substantially fewer of these strong supporters than there were even ten years ago.[11]

It is not difficult to believe that the enthusiasm for Socialism shown by the SLP's activists is not shared by the electorate and that the increasing tide of voters — especially young voters — who are moving to the National Party shows that nationalism (certainly in Scotland) now has a resonance in the electorate which Socialism had earlier in the century. To be fair to the SLP's founders, it must be remembered that they originally conceived of their party as a replacement for the Labour Party — not a long term competitor to it; thus it is not fair to tax them with looking for additional Socialist voters. But even so, the SLP's founders hoped that they might survive a Labour debacle in the next General Election with sufficient credit to rebuild the Socialist vote. I am suggesting that the research by Rose and Crewe makes even that modest hope look a bit optimistic. As Crewe argues, Labour's voters continue to vote Labour out of habit and out of a (rapidly diminishing) appreciation that Labour represents their interests — not their ideals.[12] Once

10. Rose, R. *The Problem of Party Government.*
11. Crewe, *et al.* "Partisan Realignment in Britain 1964-1974" *British Journal of Political Science* pp. 187-8.
12. *Ibid.*

broken this habitual tie even to the tepidly Socialist labour party may not be re-established by any Socialist party.

There is a way out this dark prospect for Socialists. They can argue, certainly many to the left of the Labour Party have long believed, that the reason for the electoral weakness of Socialism is the failure of the Labour Party to educate each successive generation to Socialism. The argument is that the Labour Party is too remote from the lives and struggles of most working class people, to attract them. It has, the suspicion is, been living off the ideological capital built up by the Socialist movement in the years before Labour became a majority government in 1945. It has become too closely associated with the machinery of government; too similar in government to the Tory Party; too willing both in government and in opposition to treat trade union leaders as if they were in close touch with their members. Increasingly, the argument runs, it appeals to its supporters only when it needs their votes, and treats these voters as voters only — not as workers, or residents in appalling housing, or recipients of insulting treatment at the hands of teachers, social workers, social security clerks and the nationalised industries. If this is a cogent analysis, then it might be possible for a very different kind of Socialist party to rebuild a Socialist movement which carried real conviction.

It in this light that the SLP's decision to concentrate on electoral politics — epitomised by the Darnley by-election — at the expense of other kinds of activity — such as the Moray House sit-in and the Cumbernauld dustmen's strike — was so crucial. For if the Left's analysis of Labour's failings is apt — and so many of the SLP's members were of the Left — then it is just conceivable that the SLP· was the right party at the right time and place to demonstrate it and to begin a Socialist revival. But this is a dream; for when it had the chance, the SLP was far too much like its parent to attempt anything remotely so adventurous.

Appendix A:

The Scottish Labour Party: Statement of Aims

This Statement of Aims was distributed at the Inaugural Meeting. It gives a guide to the intentions of the founders of the party.

THE SCOTTISH LABOUR PARTY

STATEMENT OF AIMS

The Aims of the Scottish Labour Party are:

To secure the establishment of a powerful Scottish Parliament to work in full Democratic partnership with the rest of the UK and represent Scotland in the Institutions of the EEC. To ensure that the Scottish Parliament is capable of applying Socialist solutions to the problems of modern Scotland.

INTRODUCTION TO THE SCOTTISH LABOUR PARTY

The Scottish Labour Party is not being formed as a temporary expedient to execute some short term political manoeuvre. Expediency and short term thinking have been the curse of the Labour Party in Scotland for far too long. The SLP has no intention of engaging in similar exercises, the situation facing Scotland now requires fundamental solutions and radical action.

The Scottish Labour Party is being created to meet this requirement; the SLP will provide a permanent political means to revitalise and modernise Socialist thinking in Scotland; it will provide Socialists with the means to shape the new Scotland which is so obviously emerging.

Profound changes are about to take place in the constitutional and economic life of Scotland. There must be created a strong Scottish Parliament with wide-ranging powers over major aspects of Scottish affairs, including the economy; this Scottish Parliament will work closely with Westminster although the precise nature of the relationship will continually change and develop in line with the growing importance of the EEC in taking decisions crucial to the planning and prosperity of the Scottish economy. The Scottish Parliament must also be Socialist to realise its full potential in improving the standard of living of people of Scotland.

Scottish Socialists must now respond to the changing situation in Scotland and take the steps which are necessary to ensure a credible position for Socialists once this powerful Scottish Parliament is established to conduct most of our affairs.

The Scottish Council of the British Labour Party, sadly, has proved itself incapable of discharging these responsibilities. The Scottish Council's "devolution policy" carries no conviction and the road followed since the October 1974 General Election has been one of retreat on the issue. In short, we all know that if the SNP were wiped out tomorrow as a political force the Scottish Council and the Cabinet would abandon devolution with joy in their hearts.

The Scottish Labour Party thus becomes the natural party for Scottish Socialists who, recognising the political realities of today's Scotland, want to see a strong Scottish Parliament created which is capable of applying in Scotland those Socialist policies that Westminster has failed to deliver.

The Scottish Labour Party will be structured quite differently from the old British Labour Party and will be no carbon copy of it. It will be a people's party, based on individual membership and individual contributions; it will be a modern Socialist party, much more democratic in its policy making and its organisation than the old Labour Party; it will be concerned to provide the maximum degree of devolution within its own ranks and will ensure that its members are the policy makers in every genuine and meaningful sense.

The Structure of the Scottish Labour party is being designed deliberately to encourage the maximum degree of free thinking and free debate. There will be a biannual Congress which will be the supreme policy making body and which will elect the party leadership; and there will be a biannual Conference which will be essentially a policy sounding body. The Scottish Labour Party will be the most advanced political organisation in Scotland.

Initially the role of the Scottish Labour Party will be to make a new and substantial policy contribution from the Scottish point of view to the ongoing debate about the future of Scotland. The SLP has already developed relationships with the industrial wing of the Labour Movement in Scotland with which it will work closely in future.

Dual membership between the Scottish Labour Party and the old British Labour Party will not be barred. However, the permanence of this arrangement will depend on whether the SLP decides to compete elect — orally with the old Labour Party. This decision is unlikely to arise as a live issue for some time but will depend in turn on whether the Labour Government continues to break its Election promises to the people of Scotland.

THE SCOTTISH LABOUR PARTY

PROPOSED REMIT FOR THE ORGANISING COMMITTEE

*Prepare Draft Rules and Constitution for First Conference

*Arrange First Annual Conference for Autumn, 1976

*Prepare Policy Discussion Papers for First Conference, Set up Constituency and Branch organisation and Head Office

*Organise Fund Raising

*Launch Membership Drive

*Develop Public Relations and establish a Journal

*Undertake Interim General management.

Appendix B:

Voting Strength of SLP Branches, October 1976

Much controversy surrounds the voting strength of delegations at the Stirling Congress. It has been unkindly suggested that the strength of the Ayrshire delegations was swollen to give the platform additional safe votes. It has also been suggested, on the other hand, that the card votes at Stirling are not a fair guide to the membership of the party because the strength of each Branch was rigorously checked by Alex Neil and all doubtful cases excluded.

This table throws serious doubts on both those positions. Branches were given one vote for each paid up member. The full annual subscription was £2. Pensioners were full members for a payment of 50p. But members were counted if they had paid the correct proportion of the Annual Subscription. Thus any non-pensioner was counted, if he had joined in January to March, and he has paid at least £1.50. If he had joined in the second quarter of the year he could be counted if he had paid £1; and 50p if he had only joined after June. Pensioners were given similar proportionate reductions. Thus it was possible to be a paid up member and be represented in one's branch's votes by paying only a quarter of the full sum.

This list does not include a figure for either Leith or Glenrothes. Both these branches were excluded from the Stirling Congress — though nothing was made of the Glenrothes exclusion. Leith had, according to its Secretary, twenty-six members. Glenrothes had four. The voting strengths of the other Branches at the Stirling Congress were as follows:

Aberdeen	46	Cumbernauld	28
Aberdeen Univ.	14	Coylton	8
Airdrie	7	Dalmellington	16
Ayr	54	Drongan	8
Auchinlech	6	Dundee Central	28
Bonnybridge	15	Dundee Whitfield	27
Catrine	12	Dunfermline	10
Clydebank	25	Edinburgh South	35
Cumnock	54	Edinburgh N. Central	65

East Kilbride	29	Oban	6
Greenock	16	Ochiltree	48
Glasgow Kelvin	30	Patna	70
South	30	Paisley	28
Pollok	22	Stewarton	14
Univ.	15	St. Andrews	18
Hamilton	10	St. Andrews Univ.	3
Irvine	6	Stirling	13
Kirkcaldy	12	Stirling Univ.	10
Leven	6	Tillicoultry	11
Motherwell	14	West Lothian	8
Moray	7		

This is a total of 883. Given that some delegation or other is inevitably absent when each vote is taken this is about what one might expect given that the highest vote at the Congress (on the Special SOC report) was 792. Within this figure 276 votes were held by the Ayrshire delegations.

Appendix C:

SLP performance in local elections

The SLP contested three local government by-elections in its first year; at Darnley in May, and at Clydebank and Irvine in September. It also contested a local government by-election in Almond ward of West Lothian in August of 1977. The results in these contests were:

Darnley May 1976

Hannigan	SNP	2126
Kelly	Labour	1369
Farrell	SLP	627
Malone	Con	358
O'Hara	Rate/payers	58

Clydebank September 1976

Butcher	SNP	299
Burke	Labour	277
Simpson	Con	178
Conroy	SLP	71
Crawford	Comm	28

Irvine September 1976

McLeod	SNP	3854
McKie	Labour	2935
Loach	Con	2531
McKay	SLP	1112

Almond Ward West Lothian August 1977

McGilliverary	SNP	917
Stenhouse	Labour	838
McLaren	SLP	44

The Party also contested a number of seats in the May 1977 District Elections.

Bibliography

A: NEWSPAPERS

Ayr Advertiser
  18 August, 1977
  5 March, 1970
  19 March, 1970

Alloa Advertiser-Journal
  12 March, 1976
  6 February, 1976
  20 February, 1976

Cumnock Chronicle
  6 March, 1970
  27 February, 1970
  13 February, 1970
  27 February, 1970
  6 March, 1970
  20 March, 1970

Daily Record
  19 January, 1975—
  18 January, 1977
  1 April, 1977
  5 March, 1970

Dunfermline Press
  13 February, 1976

The Falkirk Herald
  21 February, 1976

Forward Scotland
  Vol. 1, Nos. 1-4

Glenrothes Gazette
  4 March, 1976

Glasgow Herald
  10 December 1975—
  20 January, 1976
  21 September, 1976

Scotsman
  15 March, 1968
  12, 13 March, 1974
  11, 21, 22 March, 1975
  16 March, 1975
  5, 9, 10 June, 1975
  10 December 1975—
  22 October, 1977

Scottish Miner
  Jan. 1976

Scottish Socialist
  Issue No. 1 Oct/Nov 1976
  Special Issue November 1976
  Issue No. 5, May/June 1977

Scottish Worker
  November 1974—
  October 1977

Stirling Observer
  3 March, 1976
  6 February, 1976
  20 February, 1976

Sunday Post

  14 August, 1977

B. OTHER SOURCES: Most of these pieces are in cyclostyled form. I have deposited my copies with the Unit for the Study of Government in Scotland (University of Edinburgh). Pseudonyms are in single quotes e.g. 'Alexander James' or 'Comrade MacPherson'.

'Alexander, James', "Labouring Along the Road to Devolution", *Glasgow Herald*, 25 November, 1974.

'Alexander, James', "Labour Must Give More Power to its Scottish Elbow", *Glasgow Herald*, 26 November, 1974.

Anonymous, "SLP Contests First Elections", *Red Weekly*, 27 May, 1976, p. 5.

Armstrong, Alan, *Nationalism or Socialism: the SNP and SLP Exposed,* (a Socialist Worker Pamphlet).

Ascherson, N., "Exit the 'Entrists'", *Scotsman*, 2 November, 1976, p. 11.

Ascherson, N., "The SLP- Entrism and Counter-Measures", Memo to NOC 29 October, 1976.

Ascherson, N. "Jim Sillars: a Future Prime Minister of Scotland?", *Scotsman*, 1 November, 1975, p. 6.

Ascherson, N. "Sillars Goes It Alone", *Scotsman*, 10 June 1975.

'Comrade Ball' *Resolution on the SLP for the June Aggregate* (mimeo).

Bochel, J. and Denver, D., *Scottish Local Government Elections 1974* (Edinburgh 1975).

Brown, B. and Frame, J., *Reports to NEC on Propaganda and Publicity* 9 December, 1976 (mimeo).

'Comrade Michael Conroy' "The Political Situation and the Tasks of the SWRP" *SWRP Pre-Conference Discussion Document* (August, 1975).

'Comrade Michael Conroy' "A Transitional Approach to the Question of Government" *SWRP Pre-Conference Discussion Document* Number 2 (April, 1975).

Cook, R., "An Open Letter to Jim Sillars: No room for separatism on Europe", *Scotsman*, 17 June 1975.

Craig, F. W. S., *British General Election Manifestos 1900-74*, (London, 1975).

Drucker, H. M., "Devolution and Corporatism", *Government and Opposition*, Summer, 1977, pp. 178-193.

Eadie, Alex And Sillars, Jim *"Don't Butcher Scotland's Future: the case for reform at all levels of government"* (published privately, 1968).

Eadie, Alex; Ewing, Harry; Robertson, John and Sillars, Jim *Scottish Labour and Devolution: a discussion paper* (published privately 1974).

Easton, N., "The Defeat of the British: SLP Congress Report", *Carn*, April, 1977, No. 17, pp. 3-4.

Easton, N., The Scottish Labour Party, *Carn*, Autumn, 1976, No. 15, pp. 3-4.

Easton, N., *Socialism, Nationalism, Scotland and Independence*, (SWRP), p. 23, (January, 1975).

Edinburgh Area (SLP), *July Bulletin*, (1976), *August Bulletin*, (1976), *October Bulletin*, (1976), *November Bulletin*, (1976).

Edinburgh South Branch, (SLP) *Discussion Paper on Stirling Congress,* 10 November, 1976.

154

Farrell, Joseph, letter to Glasgow members of SLP 4 February, 1976 (also signed, without consent, by Bill Copeland and Matt McClure).

Finn, G., "A Personal Statement from a Kelvin Branch 'Trouble-maker'" intended for *Forward Scotland,* (mimeo).

Freeman, Alan *Democracy and the Scottish Labour Party* 28 May 1976. (mimeo).

Freeman, Alan *Why we need an action programme — some comments on 'Jobs and Industry'* (mimeo).

Fyfe, J. (ed). *Sentinel.*

'Comrade John Gardner' "The Evolution of Scottish Society" *SWRP Pre-Conference Discussion Document* Number 4 (July, 1975).

'Comrades John Gardner and David Johnson' "Perspectives for the Coming Year" *SWRP Pre-Conference Discussion Document* Number 3 (June, 1975).

Hood, Stuart C. D. *The Scottish Labour Party and Survey of Aberdeen Branch* (typescript available from the Politics Department of the University of Aberdeen).

IMG (Scottish Committee), *The Way Ahead for the Scottish Labour Party* (mimeo).

Johnson, R. W. and Douglas Schoen, "The 'Powell Effect': or how one man can win", *New Society*, 22 July, 1976, pp. 168-172.

James, A. & MacAllister, James, "The Scottish Labour Party", *Red Weekly*, 22 January, 1976, p. 5.

Keating, Michael, J., "Nationalism in the Scottish Labour Movement", (mimeo).

Kellas, J., "Reactions to the Devolution White Paper" in Clarke, M. G., & Drucker, H. M. *Our Changing Scotland,* (Edinburgh, 1976).

Kelvin Branch of SLP, *Minute* 28 October, 1976.

Kelvin Branch, "Who Runs Glasgow?", (mimeo).

The Labour Party, *Labour News* (October 1974).

Love, Gordon, "A Dark Day for Democracy", (Stirling University Students' Paper), Autumn Semester, 1976, p. 3.

McCabe, Bob., Letter on behalf of Cumbernauld Branch to NOC.

MacCormick, J., *The Flag in the Wind: The Story of the National Movement in Scotland,* (London, 1955).

MacKay R. & Gopsill, Tim, "Who is Funkhouser?", *The Leveller,* (Pilot Issue), p. 4.

MacLachlan, S., "From the Inside", *Daily Record,* October, 1974-December, 1976.

'Comrade MacPherson', *The Attitude of Revolutionaries to the SLP: A Preliminary Balance Sheet and Assessment,* (mimeo).

'Comrade MacPherson', *Balance Sheet and Perspectives: November 1976,* (IMG), (mimeo).

'Comrade MacPherson', *Document for April Scottish Committee (IMG): On the SLP,* (mimeo).

Martin, C. & Martin, D. "The Decline of Labour Party Membership" *The Political Quarterly* Vol 78 Number 4, October-December, 1977.

'Comrade Mills', "Resolutions For the Scottish Aggregate" (of IMG) (mimeo).

Nairn, John "Binmen Fight Wage Cuts", *Scottish Worker* (June, 1976).
Nairn, John, "Why the left was thrown out of the SLP", *The Leveller* January, 1977, pp. 24-25.
Nairn, Tom, *Comments on SLP 'Jobs & Industry' Draft Policy Statement* (mimeo).
Nairn, Tom, *Kelvinism*, September, 1976 (mimeo).
Nairn, Tom *The National Question* (mimeo).
Nairn, Tom, "Revolutionaries versus parliamentarists", *Question*, 19 November, 1976, p. 3.
Nairn, Tom, "The Scottish Labour Party", *Planet* 37/38, May, 1977
National Committee (IMG) *Minutes,* June 26/7, 1976.
Neil, Alex "A Six-Point Plan for Scottish Labour" *Courier* April 1975.
Pollock, John D., "Scottish Government Debate 1969", Speech to Scottish Council of the Labour party, (mimeo).
Pulzer, P. *Political Representation and Elections in Britain* (London, 1972).
Robertson, J., "Letter", *Scotsman*, 22 October, 1977.
Robertson, John see Eadie, Alex.
Scottish Committee of IMG, *Bulletin* New Series, Vol. 1, No. 3, 1976.
Scottish Committee of IMG, *Resolution on Forthcoming SLP Conference,* (September, 1976).
Scottish Committee of IMG, *Resolution on the SLP passed by Scottish Committee, 13.9.76 (as amended).*
Report of the Special Conference of the Scottish Council of the Labour Party 13-14 Sept., 1958.
Report of the Special Conference of the Scottish Council of the Labour Party, 1975.
Scottish Labour Party *Constitution.*
Scottish Labour Party (First Annual Congress) "Emergency Resolutions" from Cumbernauld, Kelvin, Ayr.
Scottish Labour Party, *Jobs and Industry: a Policy for Full Employment* (April, 1976), (mimeo).
Scottish Labour Party, *National Organising Committee Minutes* for: 24 January: 28 February; 3 March; 27 March; 24 April; 26 June; 17 July; 9 October; *National Executive Committee Minutes* for: 13 November; 12 December 1976; 8 January; 5 February; 6 March; and 21 May 1977.
Scottish Labour Party, *Report on the Conference held in Middleton Hall 15th and 16th May 1976.*
Scottish Labour Party *Resolutions for First Annual Congress,* September, 1976.
Scottish Labour Party, *Scottish Government* (draft discussion paper).
Scottish Labour Party, *Statement of Aims* (distributed at inaugural meeting).
Scottish Labour Party, *Widening All Our Options,* October, 1977.
SLP (Left Wing) National Council Meeting No. 2, 29 January, 1977.
Scottish Labour Party (D.W.) *Conference Bulletin,* February, 1977.
Scottish Workers Republican Party *Manifesto* (September, 1974).
'Sempreverdi, Tommaso', "Opera Buffo", *Question*, 19 November, 1976
'Comrade Shevek', *Resolution on Forthcoming SLP Conference* September 1976.

Sillars, Jim see Eadie, Alex.

Skene, Danus, *Rural Land Policy* (A discussion paper prepared for the SLP) (mimeo).

South Ayrshire Constituency Labour Party, *Minutes of G.M.C.*, 18 October, 1975.

South Ayrshire Constituency Labour Party, *Minutes of G.M.C.*, 15 November 1975.

South Ayrshire Constituency Labour Party, *South Ayr*, March, 1970.

Standing Orders Committee (of the SLP) *Report*.

Standing Orders Committee (SLP) *Special Standing Orders Report*, (October, 1976).

Scottish Workers Republican Party *Constitution*.

Williamson, Neil "Can SLP Contribute to fight Back", *Red Weekly*, 28 October, 1976, p. 7.

Williamson, Neil, "The Choice Facing the SLP: Nationalism or Class Struggle", *Red Weekly*, 11 November, 1976, p. 6.

Wilson, Brian, "Devolution is appeasement that is bound to fail", *Journalism Studies Review*, Vol. 1, No. 1, 1976, pp. 28-30.

Wolfe, Billy *Scotland Lives*, (Edinburgh, 1973).

Young, Jim, *Social Class and the National Question: the Dialectics of Scottish History*, (unpublished paper).

C. INTERVIEWS: In addition to several people who wish to remain anonymous, I have interviewed the following:

Don Allan
Neal Ascherson
Douglas Bathie
Scott Brady
Bob Brown
Norman Buchan, MP
Ray Chalmers
Alex Clark
Robin Cook, MP
Richard Cotter
Carol Craig
Derek Crossley
Norman Easton
Harry Ewing, MP
Joe Farrell
Gerry Finn
George Foulkes
Jimmy Frame
Jim Fyfe
Litster Gardiner
Jim Gibson
Douglas Gilchrist
Charlie Gordon
Dennis Gower
Sheila Gilmore
Andy Hanley
Douglas Herbison

Arnold Kemp
Bob McCabe
Eric Mackay
Stewart MacLachlan
John Mackintosh, MP
Jim Mackechnie
David McMurran
Tony Martin
Stephen Maxwell
Margaret Mellis
Ian Millar
Matt Montgomery
Roger Mullin
John Nairn
Tom Nairn
Alex Neil
John Pollock
Jimmy Reid
Don Robertson
Ed Robertson
George Robertson
David Ross
Stephen Savage
Jim Sillars, MP
Bob Tait
Neil Williamson
Jim Young